Individual Processes in Organizational Behavior

Jak Jabes

University of Ottawa

AHM Publishing Corporation
Arlington Heights, Illinois 60004

Sociol

Individual Processes in Organizational Behavior

FOR VICKY

Contents

vii

Foreword

The growing awareness of the importance of organizations in our lives has created an interest in understanding them. We are interested in individual and interpersonal behavior in organizations. We are aware that organizations influence us and that through our participation we can change organizations. We realize that organizations have subgroups, structures, and task and administrative processes. We understand that organizations are affected by technology, other organizations, and by general social and economic conditions. We also perceive that organizations can be used by their members in order to achieve personal goals.

Given the wide range of problems and issues, there are many theoretical approaches, schools of thought, and very different methods for studying organizational phenomena. This diversity has resulted in a growing, vigorous, and exciting field of study. It has also given rise to a wide variety of academic courses and research interests.

The books in this series are more than a collection of separate surveys. They have been integrated to provide a clear picture of the scope of organizational behavior, to insure consistency in approach, and to portray coherently the relationships existing across subproblem areas. Each book cross references the others, and together they provide an up-to-date working library for any person seeking to understand the field of organizational behavior.

To achieve these goals of integration and completeness, six outstanding scholars and teachers with experience teaching in business schools were assembled to write the first six books in this project. Two are social psychologists, three are specialists in organizational behavior, and one is a sociologist. The wide range of topics was first drawn up and then divided into six groups. Each of the authors then worked with the series editor to draw up a detailed outline for his or her portion of the whole work. Care was taken to insure that each author understood how he or she related to the whole series, that each author had a theme for each chapter, and that these themes were consistent within individual books and across the series as a whole. When the independent writing of each book was completed, the author and the series editor went over each manuscript painstakingly to create a solid part that was consistent with the whole series. One of the features of this series is that each book examines its topics in terms of behavioral processes. Behavior is seen in terms of complex interrelated sequences of contingent events.

Each book is written so that it can stand alone and so that it connects across the others in the series. Thus, any single book or any combination of books can be used in the classroom. In addition to the coherence of an integrated series, the integration itself helped

to reduce the length of each book and hence reduce the direct costs to the student. The
author of each book had the primary responsibility of writing on his or her assigned
topics. But when a topic from another book was
needed, the author could count on its being
adequately covered. Thus, each author could
stick to specific topics and refer to the
other books for more detailed explanations
for other topics. Together these books provide
adequate coverage of the main topics, a
compendium of ideas about organizational behavior, and a source of new ideas and critical
references.

The books in the series were written primarily for beginning M.B.A. students at a re-
spectable college or university. Some of these
schools require two semesters or three quarters
of classes in organizational behavior. For
these, we recommend that all six books be used.
Some require a semester of classes. For these
we recommend any three of the books. Those requiring one or two quarters should use two or
four of these books.

Kenneth D. Mackenzie
Lawrence, 1977

Preface

This book is an introduction to the study
of individual behavior in organizations. It
focuses on the individual and aims to explain
the processes that guide his behavior. In
doing this we have chosen to emphasize theoretical analyses and research findings from
behavioral sciences in general and from social
psychology in particular. Both are presented
topically and quite selectively. Rather than
compiling a number of research findings we
have tried to present them in order to make a
point, to clarify theory, and to advance the
understanding of the subject matter.

The book contains eight topical chapters.
Each chapter includes an introduction which
familiarizes the reader with the content of
the chapter and presents briefly our point of
view. It is impossible to reformulate theory
in an introductory text. We hope, however, that
the introduction to each chapter will reflect
our own thinking about the material covered.

The processes discussed have traditionally been studied by social psychologists. The research findings rarely deal with how these processes operate on individuals working in organizations. We believe that these are basic behavioral processes and that the general theoretical statements hold in any context. For example, the principles that explain learning would hold for children, for adolescents, and for adults whether the learning process took place at home, in school, or in an organization. Research from organizational contexts is covered whenever appropriate and available.

There are some issues that need to be elaborated in order to expose the reader to some views that will be recurring in the book. First, we shall subscribe to a cognitive view of man. This means that we shall emphasize such central processes as attitudes and expectations when explaining behavior. We do not view the infant growing up and becoming an adult by mechanistically responding to stimuli in his environment. Rather, the person transforms the external world through his cognitive structures and in turn transforms his cognitive structures to accommodate the world. Even though we have espoused a cognitive approach, it will become evident to the reader as he goes along that most of the research reported has a strong stimulus-response orientation. A stimulus-response approach limits itself only to observable stimuli in the environment and studies the person's observable responses to these stimuli. Most research, then, deals with situations where stimuli are specified and responses by human subjects recorded. Stimulus-response theorists explain behavior in simplified terms. Cognitive theorists superimpose some hypothetical constructs between stimuli and responses to explain behavior. Hypothetical constructs are variables that are not directly observable to the human eye but which are theorized to influence and guide behavior. Learning, perception, motivation, and attitudes are all hypothetical constructs.

Second, we include numerous research findings that have their origins in laboratory experimentation. The laboratory is an ideal setting to control the stimuli impinging on subjects at any given time. This has made it a popular tool for research on human behavior. The behavioral processes that we review in this book have been mostly subjected to laboratory research. The fact that most of the statements we make rest on laboratory experimentation raises a few notes of caution. One note of caution rests with the validity of our findings. Validity is the criterion by which one decides whether the researcher found what he initially set out to find. Another note of caution concerns the reliability of our findings. Reliability is the criterion by which one decides whether the findings are dependable —replicable and consistent across a variety of situations. Unfortunately, many laboratory experiments strip down the social situation that is being tested to such bare essentials that behavior as an ongoing process becomes difficult to trace.

The emphasis on laboratory research coupled with the lack of research on individual processes within organizations leads us to raise a final issue. We lack a process notion that would provide a guideline for research and stimulate more research in the field in ongoing organizations. A process explanation of behavior would try to ascertain the rules by which a system functions over time. An individual traverses through paths when he behaves. The paths can be tracked by tracing the person's past and by understanding his view of the present and his conception of the future. The paths are reached by going through stages. When studying the process we look at how different stage combinations bring about the same behavior. Tuggle (1978) and Mackenzie (1978) will have much more to say

about the notion of process. The behavioral
sciences, by and large, use simple causation
models. These models forego the notion of
process. Although most of what we review are
simple causation models we hope that we shall
instill in the reader an appreciation for the
process notion.

I would also like to take the opportunity
to thank those who had something to do with
this book. To Professor Kenneth Mackenzie, I
owe gratitude for giving me the opportunity
to write this book. His confidence allowed me
the necessary independence to write. His comments helped clear my mind about many aspects
of our discipline. Above all, his friendship
has been an extremely significant event in my
life. Another friend, Paul Swingle, provided
me with much source material for the book. The
comments by David LaMetterey and Ellen Savage
improved the book considerably. The Faculty
of Administration of Ottawa University granted
me the facilities and the time without which
this book could not have been written. Finally,
thanks are due to Louise Daoust and Michèle
Simard who typed portions of the manuscript
meeting difficult deadlines.

REFERENCES

Mackenzie, K. D. *Organizational Structures*. Arlington
Heights, Ill.: AHM Publishing Corporation, 1978.

Tuggle, F. D. *Organizational Processes*. Arlington
Heights, Ill.: AHM Publishing Corporation, 1978.

1

Learning

Learning can be defined as a change in behavior as a result of experience. It is a
hypothetical construct; that is, we never see
learning. Instead, we observe a behavior change
in an organism and infer that learning must
have taken place. Typical behavior that shows
there has been learning is called *performance*.
In social learning theory, which is the subject of this chapter, performance generally
means that momentary learning has taken place.
But according to this theory, learning can also involve long-term changes in behavior which
are not always indicated by immediate performance. As preface to a discussion of social
learning theory, we shall review the classical
and operant conditioning theories of learning
that deal only with observed behavior. Next,
some learning principles will be defined to
provide us with the necessary vocabulary.

The idea that learning can take place without its immediate effects being objectively

observed, which is the cornerstone of social
learning theory, applies to adults who constitute the sample of people studied in organizational behavior. Social learning theory demonstrates that learning takes place through observing and imitating other people. We believe that social learning theory is more in-
clusive than the classical learning theories
because it views behavior as a process and incorporates within itself the assumptions of the
classical theories.

We shall conclude this chapter by discussing
the application of learning principles in organizations, particularly in training programs
where it is most frequently used. When organizational training is explained, again the
emphasis will be on social learning theory.

THEORIES OF LEARNING

The two classical theories of learning are
classical conditioning and operant conditioning. These view man simply as responding to
stimuli in the environment and exclude from the
area of investigation any learning based on
physical maturation. Both theories incorporate
the following criteria that satisfy a minimum
definition of learning: 1) to demonstrate that
learning is taking place, the behavior observed
should be indicative of a change; 2) this
change in behavior must be relatively permanent; 3) for learning to occur some practice or
experience is necessary; 4) the practice must
be reinforced in some way.

CLASSICAL CONDITIONING

Classical conditioning tries to explain how we
learn the conditioned reflexes of the autonomic
nervous system. Although historians credit the
American psychologist Twitmyer for the first
experiments, it is the Russian Nobel Prize winner Pavlov (1927) who gave the approach promi-
nence. In his experiments with the digestive

processes, Pavlov accidentally discovered that
his laboratory dogs salivated not only when
food was placed in their mouth, but also at the
sight of food. The salivation response to food
in the mouth is a natural response; it is innate and not conditioned. Yet Pavlov noted
that even the sight of food brought about salivation. So he began experiments with food and
noted the salivation response of laboratory
dogs. He called the food the unconditioned
stimulus (UCS) and the salivation the unconditioned response (UCR). Then he paired a bell
with the food, so that the dog heard a bell
each time it was fed. After repeated trials
the sound of the bell alone caused the dog to
salivate. The dog had been conditioned to salivate to a stimulus presented in contiguity with
a UCS. The bell was called a conditioned stimulus (CS) and it gave rise to salivation, a
conditioned response (CR).

Pavlov's experiments were very important for
the development of learning theory, for they
showed how simple learning takes place and suggested clear-cut methods for conditioning animals and human beings. Experiments have since
been carried out where virtually all animal
and human subjects have been classically conditioned. It is important to note that classical conditioning does not require any rationality on the part of the organism. The nature
of the conditioning is biological and, as it
exists in nature, is tied closely to survival
functions of organisms.

OPERANT (INSTRUMENTAL) CONDITIONING

Classical conditioning explains only a small
aspect of an organism's learned behavior, since
reflexes can only account for a limited number
of behaviors. Thorndike (1911), working on responses of the skeletal musculature, found
that an animal put in a cage quickly learned
to release the door to get the food outside
the cage. He discovered that in successive
trials it took the animal less and less time

to get out of the cage. Plotting the time against trials, he obtained a learning curve. His experiments showed that the learning of a certain response was contingent on the consequences of the response. This led to the psychological principle best supported by data, known as the *Law of Effect*. This suggests that an organism will most likely repeat responses followed by satisfaction (reinforcement) and will not learn responses followed by discomfort (negative reinforcement or punishment). Obviously, this principle had been discovered long before Thorndike by animal trainers, who were getting their animals to perform tricks for a food reward.

Skinner (1938) proposed the term *operant conditioning* for the kind of learning discovered by Thorndike. When a stimulus produces a response and the response is followed by a positive consequence, over trials that response will be learned and persist even in the absence of the consequence. In this approach an organism operates on its environment to obtain a consequence. The behavior, or response, emitted is instrumental in obtaining the consequence. Instrumentality is an important notion that we shall encounter throughout this book. Skinner (1938) showed his principle of operant conditioning when a pigeon was put in what now is known as a Skinner box. The pigeon had to learn to press a lever in the box to obtain food, which was the consequence for the operant response of pressing the lever. If you wonder how information obtained with animals is used, consider gambling. A slot machine can be likened to a Skinner box. Pulling the handle provides money. Once that association is learned, it is maintained even in the absence of coins falling through the slot machine.

Operant conditioning has much wider applicability than classical conditioning. It covers many simple behaviors that we learn to perform in order to obtain rewards or avoid negative outcomes. Operant conditioning includes the range of behaviors that are voluntarily

performed for their instrumental value in obtaining a goal, while classical conditioning
relies only on involuntary responses.

PRINCIPLES OF LEARNING

Whether we describe the acquisition of a
response by classical or operant conditioning,
there are certain key principles that have to
be posited to explain why the behavior is
emitted, how it is maintained and how it is
extinguished. Generalization, discrimination,
extinction, recovery, and reinforcement will
be discussed as principles of learning. The key
principle of learning is reinforcement. Researchers have devoted more attention to the
study of reinforcement than to any other principle.

The importance of stimuli in learning cannot
be overemphasized. Learning takes place in
response to environmental stimuli. In learning
terms, a *stimulus* is any object or event, internal or external to the organism, that occasions a response. The ringing phone is a
stimulus to answer it; the oven bell is the
stimulus signaling that food is cooked. Reinforcements that control behavior are also
stimuli. Behavior is influenced by controlling
stimuli in the organism's environment. This
control can be undertaken by controlling antecedent conditions to behavior, or consequences,
each of which are stimuli.

GENERALIZATION AND DISCRIMINATION OF RESPONSES

Once a stimulus-response connection is
learned, organisms can *generalize* the bond to
other stimulus-same response linkages. In
classical conditioning generalization takes
place when a similar CS elicits the same CR.
Pavlov's dog learns to salivate to a buzzer instead of a bell. For generalization to take
place, the stimuli should be similar to the
original stimulus that gave rise to a CR. The

less similar a stimulus from the original, the less power it has to elicit the same response.

The principle of *generalization* suggests that every learning task does not have to be directly experienced by an individual. This is an important economizing construct that explains such complex learning repertoires as language acquisition. It allows for adaptations to be made by the organism to differing situations requiring the same response. A person may arrive at work punctually because it pleases his boss. He may generalize that behavior and arrive on time at all business meetings, conferences, and so on, thereby receiving the further blessings of his boss. If he transfers to another organization where tardiness is a more desired behavior, the generalization that he has made works to his disadvantage. Now he has to be able to discriminate between the responses required by the two settings.

Discrimination complements generalization. Whereas generalization is a reaction to similarities, discrimination is a differential response to stimuli. Pavlov's dogs learned discrimination when food was presented with a bell, but not with a light. Discrimination is also an important adaptive behavior. Without generalization and discrimination, organisms would have to learn a response whenever there was slight variation in the stimulus conditions. Learning principles that would be thus derived would have been so specific as to be of no value. Human beings are adaptive enough to behave according to stimulus generalization when the consequences are the same and to discriminate when consequences are different.

EXTINCTION AND RECOVERY OF RESPONSES

Removal of the consequences that maintain a learned behavior results in the weakening of the behavior and ultimately leads to its *extinction*. Pavlov's dog stopped salivating when the bell was not paired with food. In conditioning theory a behavior is maintained in an

organism's repertoire because of consequences
with which it has been paired. Removal of the
consequences results in extinction of the response. However, a response that is extinguished can be immediately relearned when the
consequences that conditioned it are again
provided. This is known as the principle of
spontaneous recovery.

Extinction is not the only way to change
conditioning. Another approach is to pair one
stimulus with another eliciting an opposite
response. This *counterconditioning* procedure works
when the new stimulus has a stronger effect on
an organism than the original stimulus. Fear
is sometimes cured by counterconditioning
procedures. If a child shows fear at the sight
of a dog, and the dog is subsequently presented
in contiguity with a chocolate bar, then the
chocolate bar could elicit a positive response,
counteracting the fear response formerly
brought about by the dog.

REINFORCEMENT

A reinforcement is anything that alters the
strength and probability of occurrence of the
response being conditioned. The UCS in classical conditioning and the consequence of a response in operant conditioning are reinforcements (commonly known as rewards and incentives). In order to obtain food the dog sali-
vates and the pigeon learns to press a lever,
because an organism tends to obtain a reinforcement that satisfies it. The Law of Effect
points out the importance of reinforcement for
learning. We learn to behave in certain ways
to obtain certain available reinforcements. As
a person matures, he[1] learns to emit the behaviors that will obtain him socially-approved
rewards. However, consequences of behavior are
not always satisfactory to the individual;
some behaviors are followed by pain and discomfort. We learn to respond to different types
of reinforcement.

TYPES OF REINFORCEMENT. Learning through conditioning is *associative learning*. Organisms learn to associate a stimulus with a response when the response is followed by a satisfying consequence. Not all responses are followed by such consequences. Sometimes the consequence is painful, at other times it can be neutral. We can classify reinforcers as being positive, neutral, or negative. A *positive reinforcer* strengthens the association between stimulus and response. Food was a positive reinforcer for Pavlov's dog. However, if an organism is satiated with food, then food loses its positive reinforcement value and becomes a *neutral reinforcer*. When people are in a deprivation situation (that is, hungry) food will be reinforcing and hence rewarding. Although food has reward value, it will not reinforce the same people when they are satiated. A *negative reinforcer* usually conditions the organism not to respond. It can extinguish the association between a stimulus and a response. A shock delivered to an animal in a cage is a negative reinforcer. This type of reinforcement is commonly referred to as a *punishment*.

Positive reinforcers can further be subdivided into primary and secondary reinforcers. *Primary reinforcers* are naturally reinforcing conditions which in themselves are satisfying. They can reduce primary motivational drives such as hunger and thirst. Food, water, and sex are primary reinforcers of a positive nature; pain is a primary reinforcer of a negative nature. Much of our behavior at early ages is under the control of primary reinforcers, but especially with maturation, secondary reinforcers come to control our behavior. *Secondary reinforcers* are learned through their association with primary reinforcers. An excellent example is money, which does not satisfy by itself but rather through what it can get for you. Money as a reinforcer controls much of individual and group behavior in organizations where one performs to obtain rewards, which are usually financial. Attention, approval, and

affection are also important secondary reinforcers of a social nature. In chapter 3 we
shall see that motivation theorists prefer to
use these social reinforcers instead of money
to influence behavior in organizational contexts.

Money is an *extrinsic reinforcer*. It is generated
outside the organism. People often respond to
reinforcers which are external to them. However, in organizational contexts the importance
of *intrinsic reinforcements* is emphasized. These
reinforcers are natural consequences of behavior as opposed to artificial reinforcers
like money. Completing a project successfully
is an intrinsic reward. The satisfaction to be
derived from finishing the project successfully maintains behavior designed to work on and
complete the project.

SCHEDULES OF REINFORCEMENT. Since reinforcements maintain behaviors and increase the
strength of desired behaviors, the way they
are administered is very important. Evidence
from general behavioral observations show that
the timing and pattern by which a consequence
follows a response is crucial. *Reinforcement
schedules* are distinguished by the number of, or
time between, nonreinforced responses, and the
regularity of the elapsed interval or time.
There are four commonly used schedules: 1) in
fixed ratio schedules a reinforcement follows a
fixed number of responses. 2) under a *fixed
interval schedule* reinforcement is provided after
a specific amount of time has elapsed after
the desired response. 3) with a *variable ratio
schedule* the number of responses between two reinforcements are determined but applied randomly. 4) under a *variable interval schedule* reinforcement varies within a variable period of
time. Ferster and Skinner (1957) discuss at
length the advantages of using partial reinforcement schedules such as those described
above. These schedules explain why many behaviors persist in the absence of reinforcements rather than being subject to extinction.

Once a habit is formed that is at least occasionally rewarded it is very difficult to change.

PUNISHMENT

Punishment is a negative reinforcer usually used to stop undesirable behavior. Although since time immemorial people have eloquently argued against punishment, it seems to be quite widespread as a technique of behavior control. Reese (1966) claims that there is general use of punishment because it immediately deters a person from making undesirable responses. Also, the person inflicting the punishment is reinforced when the undesirable behavior stops. This continues a vicious circle leading to future use of punishment. One must be careful not to define punishment as the opposite of a reward. A reward increases the probability of occurrence of a behavior; paradoxically, a punishment does not always discourage undesirable behavior. A punishment may even have the effect of increasing the probability of a response it was initially designed to decrease. For example, a supervisor may punish the leader of an informal work group who enjoys disturbing production standards; but if the group leader's peers disapprove of the production standards, then they will approve of the disruption. Punishment signals that the disruption has been successful, and to gain peer approval, the leader may step up his activities.

A negative reinforcement, such as punishment, can be administered in two ways: 1) a desired stimulus may be withdrawn, or 2) an aversive stimulus such as pain can be inflicted. For punishment to be effective, it is important that the response being punished be maintained by a positive reinforcer. The immediate effect of punishment is a drop in the frequency of the response. Continuous association of the response with the punishment should result in extinction.

The long-term effects of punishment are not always clear. Nord (1969) suggests various reasons why punishment can be an ineffective technique of behavior control. First, if punishment is perceived as a threat that exists only when the punishing agent is present, then the undesirable behavior will be maintained in his absence. Some children's behavior changes dramatically for the worse when their father goes to work. Second, punishment reduces the frequency of an undesirable response but does not necessarily give rise to the desirable behavior. Finally, punishment may lead to generalization of avoidance responses. An educational system based on punishment can create individuals who simply avoid educational settings.

As with reinforcements, punishments should follow immediately after the undesirable behavior. Care should be taken to provide an alternative response that will be reinforced once the undesirable behavior is extinguished. A complex form of learning that takes place when punishments are given is *escape-avoidance learning*. By learning to open the door, animals escape from a cage where they are being shocked. Or, they avoid receiving shocks when they learn to press a lever in the cage. People working in organizations demonstrate similar behavior when they manage to avoid meeting the boss who will have nasty things to say or when they daydream while performing a boring task.

COGNITIVE ASPECTS OF LEARNING

Conditioning theories of learning stress the organization of behavior into habits or associations. What the organism learns is stimulus-response (S-R) repertoires of varying complexity. In an approach such as operant conditioning one can specify and measure stimuli (which act as causal or independent variables) and study the results associated with these stimuli as consequents (the dependent variables).

This model does not require any mediating
variables affecting the relationship between
a stimulus and a response to that stimulus.
The organism is viewed as mechanistically responding to stimuli, often through a search by
trial and error. There have recently been ob-
jections to this mechanistic view of man from
the ranks of learning theorists. In contrast
to the strict S-R formulation of classical
learning theory, a *mediationist learning* view suggests that external stimuli (S) first give rise
to internal responses. These so-called implicit
responses (r) can be physiological (e.g., se-
cretions of the organism) or cognitive (e.g.,
thoughts and concepts). The internal response
elicits an internal cue. This cue is called an
implicit internal stimulus (s), and like the
implicit response can be physiological or cognitive. The internal stimulus triggers the
finally observable response (R). Hence, we end
up with an S-r-s-R formulation that takes into
consideration the internal processes leading to
a behavior.

That there is more to understanding behavior
than the observance of stimulus-response bonds
has its own history. In 1925 Köhler demonstrated that chimpanzees could learn to solve a
problem by "insight" rather than simple trial
and error. Although this may be taken for
granted by many of us, within learning theory
it suggests that cognitive phenomena such as
thinking and understanding, which are not observable to the human eye, are necessary mediating phenomena for certain situations. In organizational development techniques, the value
of insight is recognized, as is evidenced by
problem-solving sessions such as brainstorming.
Tolman (1948) found that rats learned to go
through a maze by learning signs. In his words,
rats learned a set of expectations or a cognitive map of their environment. His experiments led him to discover a principle known as
latent learning, in which one learns something
although there is no immediate behavioral manifestation of it. However, when the behavior is

needed it is activated from one's cognitive repertoire. To understand behavior, Tolman hypothesized that the goal-directedness of the activity had to be considered. This in turn suggested cognitions as an intervening variable. For Tolman, a cognition was an abstraction created by the theorist which partially explained behavior. The notion of goal-directedness is important, as it gives rise to a model of a person whose behavior is not merely influenced by the past but also by what he perceives the future to be. Cognitive approaches to learning take into consideration purposiveness in man. This contrasts strongly with the mechanistic model postulated by classical learning theorists.

In Tolman's view, a reinforcer facilitates performance but not learning. In latent learning experiments, rats learned a cognitive map of the maze. The addition of a reinforcement in the maze transformed previous learning into performance of a specific task. The reinforcement not only signifies observable changes in the organism in response to external stimuli, but through internal states results in creating immediately unobservable expectations for the organism. This conceptualization of reinforcement is also central to social learning theory, a recent approach which postulates that learning often takes place indirectly. As children grow up they imitate the behaviors of models in their environment. The behavior of brothers and sisters, of parents, of teachers, of classmates provide examples of desired responses. Social learning theory enlarges the classical principles of learning and incorporates cognitive mechanisms into the learning process. We shall review this theory in more detail, as it seems to be the only learning theory that bears on organizational behavior.

Social Learning Theory

Bandura (1971), criticizing the extreme

behavioristic tradition, suggests that men can learn not only by directly experiencing the consequences of their behavior but also vicariously, by observing the behavior of other people and its consequences. Building on the principles of classical and operant conditioning, Bandura establishes observational learning as a third basic learning approach. Operant learning explains the appearance of behaviors already in the repertoire of the organism. Skinner has argued that new behavior is shaped by reinforcing successive approximations of the desired behavior. According to social learning theory, this would be a tedious way to learn. More behaviors can be learned by observation than by simple trial and error and successive approximations. Cognitive mediators play a part in the observation process. Bandura incorporates informative and incentive functions of reinforcement along with response-strengthening functions. The former functions suggest that reinforcements are viewed cognitively by human beings. A reinforcement will be successful when people are aware of what is being reinforced, and when the outcome is instrumental to their needs. Awareness of what is an appropriate behavior will not produce a change in the individual when the consequence of the behavior is devalued. This point of view has also direct bearing on explanations of motivation.

An interesting aspect of social learning theory is the detailed hypotheses and research findings on imitation. *Imitation* takes place when observation of a model leads in the future to acquisition of his behavior by the observer. Bandura (1969) suggests that attention, retention, motoric reproduction, and reinforcement are the processes governing modeling. We imitate behavior that we can observe and remember to reproduce. Further, the behavior we reproduce will be governed by the skills we have acquired and the reinforcement contingencies associated with the model's observed behavior.

Social learning theory espouses a form of reinforcement that we did not previously discuss. If one can learn by observation of models and imitation of their behavior, then we have to take into consideration *vicarious reinforcement*. Observing another person rewarded or punished for his behavior can guide learning of appropriate behaviors. A *positive vicarious reinforcement* leads to an increase of the same behavior in those who have witnessed it rewarded in others. *Vicarious punishment* results when observers decrease an undesirable behavior after seeing others punished for it. This has been shown in studies of observation of aggressive behavior. In a typical study (Bandura et al., 1963), children observed models, who were either rewarded or punished for their aggressive behavior, in playing with toys. Children who watched the aggressive model being rewarded tended to imitate the model's behaviors. When the model was punished, his behaviors were not imitated. Proponents of banning violence on various media use this evidence for their arguments. They claim the media have reinforcing effects on future aggressive behavior when violence that goes unpunished is depicted on the screen. Vicarious learning does not always necessitate actual behavioral observations. As linguistic abilities develop, verbal modeling starts to substitute for behavioral modeling. Consulting an instruction manual is a good example of learning through verbal modeling.

Social learning theory relies on cognitive mediation because it posits the importance of observation, which leads to internalization of reinforcement contingencies. By identification with others in society, people not only come to imitate the behaviors of others but also to internalize their values, ideals, and attitudes. The young employee who begins to imitate the dress code and manners of the top brass of the organization soon may also begin to talk like them and to share their opinions, from political to managerial. A person imitates a model's

behavior only when either the model or his behavior is seen as relevant. Bandura suggests
three ways in which exposure to models leads
to a change in behavior: 1) Modeling effects
take place when an observer sees a model performing highly novel behaviors. If the observer is motivated, has the skills and sees
incentive value in the behavior, he can repeat
it without practice. 2) Inhibitory or disin-
hibitory effects take place when the observer
sees negative consequences to a model's behavior. Here again no learning trials are necessary, as the vicarious reinforcements are
powerful enough for learning to take place.
3) Finally, exposure to models facilitates the
expression of responses previously not displayed by the observer though already in his
repertoire.

Whereas vicarious reinforcement is important
for imitating behavior, a successful imitative
episode can trigger self-reinforcing mechanisms
in the individual. Since this is an internal
control on behavior, strict behaviorists find
it objectionable. It seems evident, however,
that a new employee, who is able to successfully reproduce skills he observes, can derive
reinforcement from his success even in the absence of external reinforcers.

By its reliance on cognitive mechanisms,
social learning theory draws attention to
selective learning. The human being attends only
selectively to his complex environment. His
thinking, emotions, perception, and motivation
influence what he will learn because he cannot
observe all stimulus-response associations
taking place in the environment. Selectivity
is a process which guides acquisition of various forms of behavior. Social learning theory
incorporates complex forms of learning. In
conditioning approaches, it is observed that
higher-order conditioning takes place when a CS_1,
giving rise to a CR_1, is paired with another
CS_2 and the latter gives rise to CR_1 later in
the absence of CS_1 (see Figure 1.1). Pavlov's
dogs were shown a light along with the bell.

Later the light alone elicited salivation. However, Pavlov could not go further than three steps. It is accepted that stimuli learned through higher order conditioning can generalize to other responses. The brain processes quite complex associations to arrive at this kind of conditioning and the original stimulus giving rise to the response is often difficult to trace. Processes of observation and imitation play an important part in acquisition of higher-order conditioning.

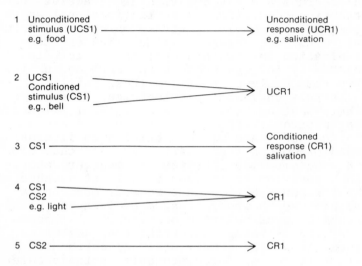

FIGURE 1.1 Higher-order conditioning.

LEARNING IN ORGANIZATIONAL SETTINGS

The learning theories that we have examined seem to receive their widest application in educational settings. Many of these principles have been tested in schools to observe their effectiveness in influencing human behavior. If one considers that joining an organization may also require some change in habitual behavior and the learning of some novel behaviors, then we can establish a direct

application for learning theory in organizations. Learning theory has been the basis for
various training techniques and principles in
industry as well as some efforts toward organizational change and development. Our concern is with individual behavior, and learning
theory best applies to individual change. Each
organization has its own culture which at the
outset dictates what novices will have to
learn. For training purposes this requires
specification of behaviors that will have to
be learned and the creation of effective
training conditions. Organizational values,
like values in all cultures, are apt to fluctu-
ate with the passage of time. Thus as an organization changes and evolves, it is often
necessary for its members to learn new skills.
Programs designed to teach these skills can
also rely on learning principles, so we find
their best application in organizational training programs.

Since adequate use of stimulus conditions and
reinforcements facilitates desired behavior,
they become important for the manager, who is
in a position to influence well-established
habits and behavior patterns. It must be
emphasized, however, that many managers use
techniques of behavior modification without
consciously being aware that they are using
them. In a study, Calvin (1962) asked his
students to reinforce students in the cafeteria
for wearing blue. Five days after the reinforcement began there was a significant increase in the number of students wearing blue.
The number of those wearing blue normalized to
before reinforcement levels when reinforcement
was stopped. Greenspoon (1955) was able to
increase the number of plural words said by a
subject by reinforcing each plural utterance
with "Mm-hmm." If simple procedures like this
can bring dramatic effects, imagine how a
manager might influence behavior by the way he
dispenses reinforcement. However, organizational settings are usually more complex environments than the laboratories of scientists.

Under laboratory control, the scientists can obtain quite powerful effects on behavior. The manager in the organization cannot control all stimuli or figure out many of the unknowns that may be affecting his workers' behavior. Quite often, however, he may find himself in control of reinforcers in an uncontaminated setting. Small-team work is a good example of a leader's reinforcement power in shaping behavior.

Psychologists have developed learning theories and tested them in their laboratories. As Bass and Vaughan (1966) concede, the application of the principles to organizational settings and training programs has taken place more or less independently of the basic research, perhaps because of the organizational practitioner's impatience. Designers of training programs are basically interested in the reinforcement of behavior to be trained, in how to transfer skills learned during training to the actual work situation, and how to distribute practice time. We shall discuss these three aspects of training programs below.

KNOWLEDGE OF RESULTS

Supervisors are interested not only in understanding behavior but also in changing it. In training one learns skills, whether they be manual or behavioral. Training programs cannot rely only on money to reinforce work habits. Money is a powerful secondary reinforcer, but oftentimes it does not come immediately to the trainee. Reinforcement schedules suggest that the best way to shape behavior is by immediate reinforcement initially. Attention and approval are more important than money as reinforcers in many training programs, as is giving the trainee information on how he is doing. *Knowledge of results*, or feedback, is very helpful in modifying behavior. Feedback functions as a reinforcement and also allows the trainee to correct and improve his behavior. Even if the trainee is quite motivated to learn, without any feedback on how he is doing, his performance will be set back. Miller (1965) demonstrated the importance of knowledge of results in a training program. In the first stage of training, workers did not receive any positive feedback. In further stages, standardized feedback, both positive and negative, was given. Performance improved dramatically in the latter stages of training.

Feedback on performance can take varied forms as shown in Figure 1.2. It can be quite *specific* or *general*. It can be given immediately after performance, called *augmented feedback*, or with some time-lag after performance, called *summary feedback*. Important to feedback is that it can be either *intrinsic* or *extrinsic*. Intrinsic feedback has more value because it sets the person to be self-reinforced. The knowledge of having succeeded works in itself as a reinforcer, thus motivating the person to keep up his successful behavior. Ammons (1956) says that the effect of providing knowledge of results is an increase in motivation to learn. This is true especially if the information is given without delay and is specific. It is unfortunate that in most organizations knowledge of results is not given to employees often enough to produce useful results. Frequently the yearly evaluation is merely a summary feedback so impersonal and standard that it does not help correct behavior or motivate the employee.

TRANSFER OF TRAINING

A major problem with training may be that it takes place in an environment different from the one to which the trainee will return. Many off-the-job training programs have the difficult task of ascertaining that training will be transferable to the on-the-job situation. The principles of generalization and discrimination suggest that people will be able to respond in the same fashion to similar cues, and differentiate between similar cues requiring differential responses. However, even

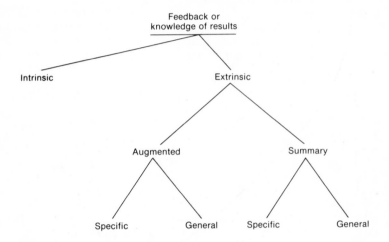

FIGURE 1.2 Forms of feedback.

though the discriminative ability is there,
the training might be useless. A trainee who
has participated in a program to improve his
decision skills will quickly learn not to make
decisions in his own office if his boss dislikes his behavior. What is learned in training will be best transferred to the actual job
if stimuli and responses are similar in training and on the job. Task similarity facilitates
transfer, but the manager can also play a part
by clarifying similarities and differences of
the task on the job with the one during training. Transfer can be positive where what is
learned during training generalizes to the job.
Transfer can also be negative where learning
during training inhibits performance on the
job. Or it can have no observable effect.
Identical stimuli lead to high positive transfer because generalization is at its easiest.
Figure 1.3 shows the hypothetical relationship
between stimulus similarity and positive transfer.

   The on-the-job training techniques of job-
instruction training, apprentice training,

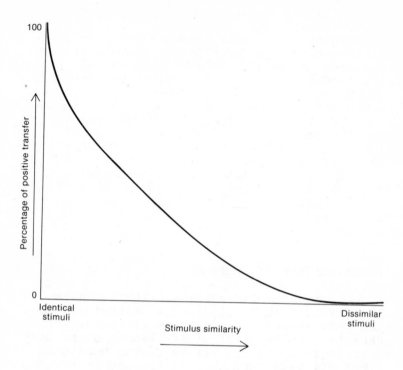

SOURCE: B. M. Bass and J. A. Vaughan (1966), p. 39.

FIGURE 1.3 Hypothetical curve depicts the relationship between stimulus similarity and amount of positive transfer when responses are the same.

assistantships, internships, job rotation, and coaching seem more favorable for transfer of learning than off-the-job training techniques. Even though off-the-job training programs suffer from the fact that the skills learned often are not transferable to the job, the programs are practical because they are varied in kind and offer training that would be too expensive for a company to undertake within itself. The worth of the programs lies more in the kind of training they offer.

PRACTICE IN TRAINING

Learning principles are used in training to achieve a desired performance competence for trainees. Although rapid and economical training is desirable, skills and behaviors cannot always be learned quickly. Different jobs require different schedules of practice. Learning theorists have devoted a great deal of attention to a problem called *part versus whole learning*. Briefly, the question is whether it is best for practice to be massed in a concentrated time period or distributed over long periods of time. The nature of the skill to be learned usually dictates whole or part learning. Generally distributed practice is preferred to massed practice, except for complex problem solving. When difficult tasks are undertaken, the whole method is used with incorporating part methods within it. If tasks are fatiguing, distributed practice is more advantageous. However, for tasks that involve meaningful verbal material, distribution of practice results in loss of interest. A compromise between part and whole methods would suit most learning tasks. Whole, part, and the combination of whole and part training are exemplified below:

Method	*Period 1*	*Period 2*	*Period 3*	*Period 4*
Whole	$A+B+C$	$A+B+C$	$A+B+C$	$A+B+C$
Part	A	B	C	$A+B+C$
Whole and Part	A	$A+B$	$A+B+C$	$A+B+C$

The application of learning theories to training has been of greatest interest to industrial psychologists. What has been presented is a very brief overview of the field, as the whole spectrum of training activities is outside the scope of this chapter. Simmons (1978) also deals with training (see chapter

5). Nevertheless, we would like to emphasize
that many training programs rely on principles
of learning theory where they allow trainees to
learn by observing trainers or other trainees.
Vicarious reinforcement is provided by observing a trainee being rewarded for successful
accomplishment of a skill. This is why we feel
that social learning theory has the most to
contribute to organizational training programs.

THE MAN IN THE GRAY FLANNEL SUIT

The "organization man" wears colorful double
knits these days. His hair is longer than in the
early fifties, and chances are he sports a
moustache and/or sideburns. Changes in dress
codes of organization men are rooted in changes
in values and attitudes of society at large.
Many things have changed since the passage of
the man in the gray flannel suit. The diffusion
and adoption of new organizational fashions can
also be explained in learning terms. The reinforcements for wearing colorful suits are
there. But let us be cautious with our organization man when explaining his behavior in the
language of learning. Man is a complex social
animal, and it is both difficult and dangerous
to apply to him all the learning principles
developed with animals. Positive reinforcement
rather than negative reinforcement is usually
more conducive to desired behavior. It is
also more consistent with humanitarian values
held in most industrial societies. And even if
we see behavior modification as a dangerous
tool developed by psychologists and available
to managers to condition or brainwash, let us
not forget that the employee can shape his
supervisor's behavior, too. Behavior modification is a two-way street.

NOTES

[1]Throughout the book, the author refers to managers,
other business personnel, experimental subjects, and so

on, as "he." This is done for the sake of brevity, and the reader should understand that the reference is to both women and men.

REFERENCES

Ammons, R. B. "Effects of Knowledge of Performance: A Survey and Tentative Theoretical Formulation." *Journal of General Psychology 54* (1956): 279-99.

Bandura, A. *Principles of Behavior Modification.* New York: Holt, Rinehart and Winston, 1969.

_____. *Social Learning Theory.* New York: General Learning Press, 1971.

Bandura, A.; Ross, D.; and Ross, S. A. "Imitation of Film-mediated Aggressive Models." *Journal of Abnormal and Social Psychology 66* (1963): 3-11.

Bass, B. M., and Vaughan, J. A. *Training in Industry: The Management of Learning.* Belmont, Calif.: Wadsworth Publishing Co., 1966.

Calvin, A. D. "Social Reinforcement." *Journal of Social Psychology 66* (1962): 15-19.

Ferster, C. B., and Skinner, B. F. *Schedules of Reinforcement.* New York: Appleton-Century-Crofts, 1957.

Greenspoon, J. "The Reinforcing Effect of Two Spoken Words on the Frequency of Two Responses." *American Journal of Psychology 68* (1955): 409-16.

Köhler, W. *The Mentality of Apes.* New York: Harcourt, Brace and World, 1925.

Miller, L. *The Use of Knowledge of Results in Improving the Performance of Hourly Operators.* General Electric Company, Behavioral Research Service, 1965.

Nord, W. R. "Beyond the Teaching Machine: The Neglected Area of Operant Conditioning in the Theory and Practice of Management." *Organizational and Human Performance 4* (1969): 375-401.

Pavlov, I. P. *Conditioned Reflexes.* Translated by G. V. Anrep, London: Oxford University Press, 1927.

Reese, R. P. *The Analysis of Human Operant Behavior.* Dubuque, Indiana: William C. Brown, 1966.

Simmons, R. E. *Managing Behavioral Processes: Applications of Theory and Research.* Arlington Heights, Ill.: AHM Publishing Corporation, 1978.

Skinner, B. F. *The Behavior of Organisms.* New York: Appleton, 1938.

Thorndike, E. L. *Animal Intelligence.* New York: MacMillan, 1911.

Tolman, E. C. "Cognitive Maps in Rats and Men." *Psychological Review* 55 (1948): 189-208.

2

Social Perception

Perception is the primary mechanism by which humans come to know the world. It can be termed a translational process, whereby what is "out there" impinges through the eyes to the central nervous system, resulting in an *impression* of the initial reality. We emphasize the word "impression" because what takes place in the nervous system (the image translation) is not a completely mechanical process, but one which the individual influences in his own unique way. The perceptual process as it takes place cognitively within the organism is inferred; it is not observed. The response made by the individual suggests to us how the objective reality "out there" has been distorted.

Perception was initially studied in terms of how people perceived inanimate objects. An important notion that emerged from early research was that perception was selective. We shall briefly explain principles of perception derived from these early studies. However, our

27

interest lies in social perception. Our emphasis will be on how we perceive other human beings, for people are at the core of social perception. Two issues are raised when we discuss person perception: 1) how accurate are our perceptions of others, 2) how we combine information about others to arrive at an impression of them. This latter issue paves the way for the implicit personality theory which elaborates how each individual arrives at unique ways of forming and using impressions.

A great deal of interesting laboratory research on perception is reviewed in this chapter. Nevertheless, social perception takes place daily within the environments in which we live. These environments are more complex and subject to more uncontrollable influences than the psychological laboratories. Many elements do influence our perceptions in our everyday encounters—an important one is culture. Membership in a culture means using a common language and sharing common values. We shall show how these factors influence social perception.

The perceptual process emerges as the basis of our social behavior. People form impressions through which they come to know the world in categories and structures that are often quite simple. The categories and structures they develop to make sense out of perceptual phenomena in turn provide them with a frame of reference against which to judge new perceptions. This frame of reference forms the background for communication and interaction with other people.

PERCEPTUAL ORGANIZATION

When you walk into an office, you perceive a desk, rather than its color, shape, or uses. The various physical properties of an object are grouped and seen as a coherent, organized unit. This notion that perceptual phenomena are organized in holistic patterns dates back to the Gestalt psychologists' school of perception, which has identified various principles that apply to the perception of objects.[1]

The most important of these principles is that our perceptions are organized and have a structure. We do not simply perceive unrelated colors and patterns of lines; instead, we give structure to these impressions and see a desk. The various parts that go into making a desk give us a whole perception, that of the desk. This whole is something above and beyond the parts. Simply putting the parts together does not give us the perception. The Gestalt school would say that the whole is different from the sum of its parts. One reason why we organize and structure our perceptual experience is that perceptual phenomena display constancy. Regardless of the illumination in an office, the desk is perceived as a desk. Its image has been imprinted, and experience with desks makes the object you see in the room a desk, irrespective of illumination intensity. Objects have size, shape, color, and location constancy which allow people to see them as the same object under differing conditions. We come to experience perspective as a variation, but it does not influence our perception of size. An image forms in the eye when we see two objects of the same size far apart. The one closer to the eye is bigger; in reality, we adjust our perception to take into consideration size constancy.

Another reason we impose structure on perceptual phenomena is that these phenomena often appear in patterns. One example of such pattern would be a *figure-ground relationship*. This happens when a pattern emerges as a figure against an extended background (see Figure 2.1).

Most introductory texts of psychology abound with visual examples of what we have tried to explain in a few sentences, and the interested reader can consult them for more information.[2]

Constancy and patterning give perceptual phenomena structure and stability. Furthermore, our active involvement in the perceptual process by structuring the phenomena allows us to give meaning to our perceptions. This meaning derives from our own experiences with the objects of perception and their relationship to other objects.

FIGURE 2.1 The figure-ground relationship. What is taken as ground determines the figure perceived.

SELECTIVITY IN PERCEPTION

We have introduced perception as a process whereby the reality "out there" is translated into coherent, holistic, structured, stable impressions. But, there is too much "out there" to see. It is impossible to attend to all stimuli impinging on our senses. Our perceptual processes are *selective*. We can pay attention only to certain stimuli at any given moment. This context has three key aspects: 1) the properties of the object that is being perceived; 2) the properties of the perceiver himself; 3) the total situation in which the object appears. We have already discussed how patterning such as figure-background relationships, which make up the total situation, lead to the structuring of perceptions. We now turn to the first two aspects that influence selectivity.

STIMULUS PROPERTIES INFLUENCING PERCEPTUAL SELECTIVITY. Value, meaning, familiarity, and intensity are important properties of the object of perception that can influence selectivity. Objects that have value can command our attention, and in turn value may lead to distorting the object of perception. In a classic study Bruner and Goodman (1947) asked children to adjust a circle of light to the subjectively perceived size of coins that they held in their hands. It was found that the children adjusted the circles to correspond to the value rather than the size of the coin. Furthermore, lower-class children overestimated valuable coins even more than middle-class children did. This phenomenon has been labeled *perceptual accentuation*.

Through our socialization we come to learn to associate emotional meaning with objects. The sight of an almond chocolate bar gives rise to pleasant feelings in my body. The almond chocolate bar stands out very easily as a figure in the varied background of a candy store. Unlike the almond chocolate bar, some objects disturb us. Objects laden with emotionally disturbing properties have been observed to create what are called *perceptual defenses*. McGinnies (1949) found an interesting way in which selectivity affects emotionally disturbing perceptual phenomena. He showed female subjects socially taboo words and asked them to identify the words. During the experiment, he monitored their emotional reactions by an electronic method measuring the galvanic skin response (GSR). He found that these stimuli were more easily recognizable than stimuli for which the emotional response was neutral, but they were eliciting substitute responses which acted to prevent the recognition of the taboo word. The GSR, however, recorded the emotional reaction showing that the taboo word was recognized. Perceptual defense seems to exist in people. People who deny certain emotions in themselves have a tendency to be blind and insensitive to the same emotions in others.

The more familiar we are with an object, the more easily it is recognized. Familiarity can influence selectivity in two ways: 1) we recognize a familiar object amidst a multitude of new and strange objects; 2) in a place full of familiar objects, something novel catches our attention.

Subliminal perception (that is, perception that is below the threshold of awareness) has interested people in the field of marketing. It is hard to determine how intense the presentation of an object has to be before we direct our attention to it. Evidence shows that objects presented subliminally can be accurately perceived. However, high intensities above this threshold usually are necessary for effective perception.

PERSON PROPERTIES INFLUENCING PERCEPTUAL SELECTIVITY. The perceptual response made by an individual is not simply a result of the objects "out there." The external stimuli impinging on his central nervous system are affected by his internal states (such as his feelings, emotions, needs, attitudes) in producing a response. For example, perceptual defense is also a person property influencing selectivity. When a person distorts a word like "whore" to another like "where," it may be because of a certain type of upbringing and feelings.

The preoccupations of an individual while perceiving something will usually influence his perception of it. Momentary needs can become very salient and distort perception. In pioneering studies Levine et al. (1942) studied groups of individuals deprived of food for different lengths of time. Their subjects were shown ambiguous drawings through a glass screen and asked to associate each drawing with a word. They found that the longer the subjects were deprived of food the more food-related responses were given to the ambiguous stimuli. This is an example where a perceptual response suggests what the internal state of the responding person is.

We have said familiarity with an object influences selectivity. A person becomes more selective to the degree that a learning history is associated with the object of perception. Objects that in the past have been associated with rewards are selected rather quickly as opposed to those that have been coupled with punishments. In the language of the preceding chapter, one can say that we form perceptual habits.

The culture at large, of which a person is a part, also influences his perception. Groups within a culture have normative power over the behaviors of their members. The nonmaterial culture with its language, legal system, and traditions creates a compelling frame of reference for perception. In the last section of this chapter we shall deal with the effects of culture on perception.

PERSON PERCEPTION

Person perception follows the same principles outlined for object perception. However, the process raises an intriguing issue: a perceiver (P) is aware that the perceived person (O) is himself a perceiver. As opposed to simply observing an inanimate object, a psychological transaction takes place between P and O, where each is aware of the other and each tries to understand the other's perceptions, needs, and attitudes. This dual active interchange in the person perception process is very important. Hastorf et al. (1970) suggest two crucial facets of our experience of other people. First, we perceive others as causal agents. We think of them as controlling their behavior in such a way that at any time they can intend to do things and realize these intentions through their behavior. People as objects of perception can affect their environment. Second, we perceive people as being similar to ourselves. By this kind of perception we go beyond the mere observation of their outward appearances and behaviors and try to infer their internal states. When we perceive a smile, we infer the emotional state as one of happiness.

Historically, three areas have been investigated in person perception. Early studies tried to ascertain the accuracy of the perception. Later studies focused on the nature of the impression obtained. More recently attention has turned to attributional processes by which we come to infer the dispositional properties of others. The attention here is more on the causal agent aspect of people. We shall review the accuracy and impression formation notions next, and attempt to explain attributional processes in chapter 6.

ACCURACY IN PERSON PERCEPTION

Early interest in person perception focused, oddly enough, not on the explanation of person perception, but on finding out how accurate people were in their perceptions of others. An attempt was made to find if some people were better perceivers than others, and if so, what were their characteristics. It was felt that accurate perceptions could make people more effective in certain positions, such as leadership. Research, however, has been inconclusive on this issue. Accurate social perceptions do not necessarily lead to better interpersonal adjustment. Steiner (1955) proposed that accurate social perceptions would be beneficial to interpersonal relationships if the participants were cooperatively motivated, if behaviors that were actually perceived were relevant to the relationship, and if participants could freely alter their behaviors based on their perceptions. The notion of accurate perception immediately raises the question of finding criteria that explain what is "out there." That is, if we are to make an impression, our inference would have to be validated against some objective criteria of the reality. With people as objects of perception, this creates some difficulties.

One line of studies on accuracy in person perception is tied to Darwin's (1872) work. Darwin had suggested that facial features are biologically characteristic of species and reflect internal emotional states. However, research has failed to show that people can identify which features are associated with which emotional states. Efforts to distinguish dimensions necessary to describe discriminable facial expressions have resulted in an evaluative dimension such as pleasant-unpleasant (Schlosberg, 1952). We shall encounter an evaluative dimension quite often in describing psychological phenomena. There are various reasons for the lack of identification of other dimensions. People may express the same emotion in different ways. Photographs which have been used as stimuli in these studies are too static in comparison to real life encounters with people, where various cues besides facial ones are utilized to form an impression.

The central question regarding internal states, such as emotions, is whether people express the same emotion by highly similar facial cues or whether there are gross variations in facial representations of the same emotion. Even though this question remains unanswered, the real concern with accuracy in person perception is related to identifying those people who are good judges of personality traits. The interest here has been in finding out how people's impressions of others match with validity criteria. In experimental work people were usually asked to rate others using descriptive adjectives and personality descriptions. The accuracy of the description was determined by a discrepancy score computed by comparing the person's impression with a validity criterion, which could be the self-description of the rated individual or the judgment of an expert such as a clinical psychologist. Cronbach (1955) criticized these approaches because of their faulty methodologies. He suggested that perceivers can be biased in various ways and that different accuracy scores would be necessary for different biases. Cronbach's critique specifically suggested that people may have interesting ways by which they map together traits about others, which give us more information on *how* they know the world rather than how *accurately* they know it. For example, someone given a number of traits such as good-honest-healthy-handsome may infer that the stimulus person is also intelligent. Of interest is the fact that he may be associating intelligent with one of the given traits, say honest, and use this implicit correlation constantly. We could learn something about his implicit impressions in this way; however, it does not tell us much about the accuracy of his perception. By looking at studies on accuracy one could conclude that all people are accurate some of the time, and that probably is what one would expect anyway. Interest has focused more on how we combine various cues to form an impression about another person.

IMPRESSION FORMATION

Being accurate in perceiving others may have its merits, but it is more interesting to find out how people combine perceptual information to form impressions of others. This area of investigation has been of recent interest to researchers. What we try to look at in impression formation is the perceiving person's knowledge processes. These processes lend themselves to investigation neatly if we accept as a departure point the assumption that perceptual phenomena have organization. Just as we fill in missing parts when we perceive objects, we do the same thing when we perceive people. On the basis of a few characteristics we verbalize our impressions of others. Most people will tend to believe you should not arrive at an impression of another with only scant information about the other. When asked to do this people perhaps tend to resist in order not to look bad. But the evidence seems to show that a universal tendency exists to make first impression judgments based on few characteristics. Furthermore, one interesting aspect of this impression is its tendency to be consistent. When perceiving an office building, you can differentiate various evaluative attributes about it. You can like the entrance, but dislike the paint in the halls, and so on. When forming impressions of people we try to arrive at a consistent overall evaluation rather than see the person as good and bad, beautiful and ugly. An impression always results in an evaluation. This evaluative dimension basically captures all that goes on about the process of person perception.

The advantage to the individual of the first impression is its economy. Based on one or two sweeping judgments we can further interact with another person without having to judge him constantly. A bias associated with this kind of economizing is known as *temporal extension*. This refers to the process whereby a momentarily perceived characteristic of the person is assumed to be permanent. This makes sense when we also know that we tend to perceive others as consistent, in other words, as constant entities.

It was Asch (1946) who pioneered impression formation studies by using a Gestalt formulation. The Gestalt school had postulated that a perception as a whole is not a sum of its parts. Asch maintained that the same principle held for impression formation. He reasoned that when we form impressions we simply do not add a known number of attributes about a person and arrive at a final impression, which as an evluation reflects the sum of the attributes. In his classic study he presented two groups of subjects with descriptions of a stimulus person to be judged. Each group received the same six traits and one different trait. The person was described as intelligent, skillful,

industrious, warm, determined, practical, and
cautious to one group. For the second group,
"warm" was replaced with "cold." Each group
wrote sketches about the stimulus person and
also selected traits from a list that fitted
their impressions of the person. Asch obtained
very different results from the two groups.
The warm group saw a happy, generous, good-
natured person, whereas the cold group perceived the stimulus person as more selfish. If
people simply added the traits this result
would not have been obtained. Based on variations of the design, Asch argued that warm and
cold were central traits. By *central traits* he
referred to those traits which explain how most
other traits are combined to form an impression. Warm and cold are central traits in the
sense that they guide the organization of the
impression. Support for Asch's findings has
come from several replications. Kelley (1950)
introduced a lecturer to two classrooms using
identical descriptions of the person with the
warm-cold difference. Students were more willing to interact with the lecturer when he was
introduced as a warm person than when he was
introduced as a cold person. Students were
then asked to make impressions of the lecturer's traits. The differences in the impressions
of the lecturer were similar to Asch's results.
  Impressions are usually based on our past
experiences. Categories that we are familiar
with are resurrected to deal with new perceptual phenomena. Haire (1955) provided a
group of union members and personnel men from
industry with pictures of two men. With the
exception of their careers, the descriptions
of the men in the pictures were identical. In
half the cases, the man in the picture was described as treasurer of the union, in the other
half, as the local manager of a small plant.
The two groups of subjects, when asked to check
through descriptive adjectives, arrived at
radically different impressions depending on
whether the person in the photo was identified

as a union man or a management member. Also,
labor and personnel subjects arrived at different impressions. We see here how past
categories of knowledge are applied to form
impressions. We shall also encounter this process when we describe stereotyping behavior.

What stands out in these studies is the
interaction among traits. Two people may be
perceived to have intelligence, but the meaning
of intelligence when it interacts with other
perceived traits may change from one person to
another. For example, one person is perceived
as intelligent and industrious and another as
intelligent and lazy. In this case, the quality
of intelligence in the two individuals is not
perceived in the same way.

The way by which people combine traits also
accentuates several perceptual biases. Some of
these biases have been identified and studied.
A typical perceptual bias is the *halo effect.*,
which means that one person judges another
solely on terms of good or bad. All of the
subject's other characteristics and qualities
are generated from these two qualities. The
halo effect suggests that people will spread
a favorable impression about another person to
certain other attributes. For example, a
beautiful woman may be seen as more intelligent
and more emotionally secure because of a halo
effect caused by her beauty. Another bias is
termed *logical error*. It is similar to the halo
effect and means that a person who knows some
of a subject's personality traits will infer
others that he has no certain knowledge of. For
example, a wealthy politician may be considered
more honest and less ambitious than an impover-
ished one. These inferences follow constructs
and hypotheses that the person has acquired
about others. Finally, *positivity bias* refers to
the tendency to systematically evaluate others
more in positive than in negative ways. We
shall now see how these biases enter impression formation in a process called *implicit
personality theory*.

IMPLICIT PERSONALITY THEORY

Asch's work has been responsible for a lot of speculation on processes of impression formation. A key question researched by Asch was the relationship between the stimulus and the perceptual response made to it. Given some cues about the person, Asch was trying to find out how we generate an impression, how we supply what is missing, filling in details in some fashion. Bruner and Tagiuri (1954) coined the term "implicit personality theory" to describe how we generate inferences about others. They suggested that human beings have developed a common-sense or naive approach by which each systematically combines and associates traits. Just as a medical doctor combines cues to arrive at a diagnosis, so a person combines cues to arrive at an impression. The doctor does not arrive at his diagnosis randomly; he follows medical theory. The same applies to the person arriving at an impression. He follows his own implicit personality theory. The person has his own set of constructs that: 1) define phenomena, 2) make assumptions about behavior, and 3) develop hypotheses linking the concepts. When he observes someone's behavior, or learns some attributes of another person, the observer uses his implicit personality theory to infer the trait he does not know. Implicit personality theory studies both what and how impressions result.

Asch had suggested how perceptions of central traits lead to inferences about other traits. Wishner (1960) provided the hard data to explain how certain perceived traits lead to definite impressions. Wishner showed that if one knew how traits were related to each other, one could predict response traits from stimulus traits. He also showed that traits became central because they correlated highly with response traits. This was different from Asch's point. It has also been argued that the context can influence which traits will be central. Sometimes the meaning of a trait is

modified to fit it to other bits of known information about the stimulus person. These efforts seem to be related to producing a consistent impression (Kaplan, 1971). It is this
relationship among traits that we call the
implicit personality theory.

Studying how an impression is made clarifies
the cognitive processes by which information is
combined. One line of study here has been the
order of presentation of the stimulus material.
When we meet someone, what impresses us about
him—what characteristics do we notice first
or last? In psychological parlance this is
known as *primacy* and *recency effects*. A primacy effect occurs when information presented first
about a person influences the total impression.
Conversely, a recency effect takes place when
the information presented last influences the
impression most. Luchins (1957) found that when
positive information about a person was presented before negative information subjects
rated the person more favorably than those
reading the descriptions in reversed order.
He also showed that this primacy effect can be
reduced by providing a warning not to judge too
hastily and by requiring other activities between judgments. In general, whether a primacy
or recency effect is obtained depends on the
total situation.

Another line of study has focused on factors
affecting the evaluation of the final impression. Is it arrived at by adding up the evaluations of each stimulus trait or by taking an
average? The two models exist, each with its
proponents, and the debate has been unresolved
for some time. Triandis and Fishbein (1963)
adhere to a summation model. They suggest that
the final evaluation can be derived from the
sum of the component traits. They showed that
their subjects used this model when evaluating
a stimulus person. Anderson (1962) first proposed a simple averaging model where the final
evaluation is equal to the sum of component
traits divided by the number of traits. Later
Anderson (1968 a, b) provided a weighted average

model to account for the initial favorability
of traits along with their combinational mix.

CULTURAL CONTEXT OF PERCEPTION

We grow up, not in isolation, but rather immersed in a culture. Social scientists use
varying definitions of culture to suit their
needs. For our purposes we can define *culture*
as the man-made part of the human environment.
This definition incorporates not only the
material features of the human environment, but
also the nonmaterial aspects, such as the
language, the science, the religion, and the
laws of a people. There is probably no doubt
that a given culture influences the perceptions
and behaviors of its members. If being a member
of a culture results in perceptions of the same
reality different from nonmembers' perceptions,
then it will be fruitful to explore the ways in
which culture affects perceptions. We believe
that the language used, the values shared by
the culture, and membership in organizations
all influence our perception.

Tajfel (1969) identifies three categories of
cultural variables that affect perceptual responses. The first is *functional salience*, which
means that our particular ecological environment influences the perceptual discriminations
we learn. An islander and a desert dweller
would each perceive and react very differently
to the sea and the sand. The second variable
is *familiarity*. Living in one culture as opposed
to another increases exposure to certain objects. Various studies confirm that the level
of familiarity one has with certain man-made
artifacts can influence his perceptions.
Segall et al. (1966) studied various cultures
by exposing them to perceptual illusions. It
was found that cultures familiar to a square
world of right angles were susceptible to an
illusion like the Mueller-Lyer (Figure 2.2),
whereas African tribes living in round huts
did not perceive the illusion. *Systems of*

communication is the third variable. Language is
a good example of this, and we turn to a more
detailed analysis of its influence on perception.

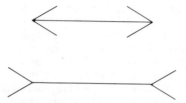

FIGURE 2.2 The Mueller-Lyer illusion. Although the bot-
tom line looks longer than the upper line they are
actually the same length.

LANGUAGE AND PERCEPTION

A child is socialized within his cultural
context. An important tool used by the culture
to socialize the child is language. Language
in turn affects his cognitions, which allow
him to know the world around him. When he perceives the world, he provides input for his
cognitions.

There is a historical tradition going back
to the Greek philosophers that ties together
language and cognition. More specifically, it
has been maintained that language may directly
influence our cognitions. An interesting viewpoint of the anthropologist Sapir (1912) has
been translated by Whorf (1956) to a hypothesis
regarding perception, cognition, and language.
Known as *Whorf's linguistic relativity principle*, the
hypothesis claims that the world view of individuals in a particular culture depends on
the structure and characteristics of the
language that they speak. In this deterministic
approach, Whorf suggests that when a person is
born into a culture, the language system of
the culture is imposed on him. The grammatical
structure of the language shapes the experiences of the person in a deterministic way. By

learning a language we come to view the world in a particular manner. In other words, people do not live in the same world and simply label things differently; rather, they live in different societies, each a distinctive world. To support his contentions, Whorf provides anthropological data in which he compares languages that have different grammatical structures. Good experimental tests of the hypothesis are very difficult to devise. The best approximations are studies by Ervin-Tripp (1967) on bilingualism. She gave bilingual Japanese women several psychological tests, and found that their responses matched more closely responses of unilingual Japanese women or unilingual American women depending on the language they used to answer the test items.

Whorf's hypothesis is interesting, but the evidence is not rigorous enough to rule out other possible explanations which might account for differences in grammar without supporting the hypothesis of a widely different cognitive process. One could equally well espouse an opposite view, where language is seen as determined by one's total environment. In this view, language evolves out of our experiences with the environment. Eskimos use many more words to describe snow because their environment allows them to differentiate subtleties in snow that we cannot see because we never experience snow as they do. Arabs use many different terms to denote a camel. Cultural interchange, whether it is because of diffusion or due to a nation's being conquered, results in one culture adopting new terms nonexistent in its own language to deal with new experiences.

These two views seem at best to complement each other. They both suggest that culture and language play an important mediating role in helping us to learn and know the world. Our everyday perceptions and thoughts are frequently influenced and molded by our immediate surroundings, of which our culture and language are a part.

PERCEPTUAL BIASES ARISING FROM ONE'S CULTURE

When discussing impression formation, we described situations where people arrive at a whole perception of a person based on a number of given traits about him. One effect of living immersed in different enclaves of culture is that sometimes we are confronted with single items of categorical information about others (that another person is, for example, a Jew, a black, a Chinese) and we quickly provide a strong evaluation based on this information. This culturally mediated perception is called *stereotyping*, a term coined by the late Walter Lippmann (1922). These ethnic categories can evoke very strong evaluations in the absence of other information about the person. Stereotyping is often related to prejudice. *Prejudice* is an attitude that predisposes one to react favorably or unfavorably towards a group or its members. Prejudice in turn can be translated into a stereotyped perception of a member of an ethnic group. It is important not to fall into a trap here and assume that all prejudices consist of unfavorable attitudes, and that it is a bad thing to stereotype people. While in everyday language, prejudice and stereotyping carry negative evaluations, one can be positively prejudiced towards his loved ones. Stereotyping, regardless of the nature of the perception, is held for reasons of economy. In a sense, stereotypes that we have about members of other ethnic groups replace first impressions. A negative stereotype, obviously, would prevent us from further interaction with someone that we might have liked. Perhaps this is the price we have to pay for living in an overly complex environment.

Secord and Backman (1974) outline three processes that take place in the act of cultural stereotyping. First, people identify a category of persons. This categorization can be based on physical characteristics such as sex or age, or on membership to a group or nation. Categories such as women, old men, Chicanos,

and hippies are highly visible. Second, within
the culture there must be some consensus on
the traits to be attributed to the category of
persons. An early study by Katz and Braly
(1933) suggested that such agreement existed
among students at Princeton. One hundred students were presented with ten ethnic groups
and 84 adjectives and asked to check those
words that characterized each ethnic group.
The study was replicated several times at
Princeton and showed that the consensus existed
even though the nature of the trait groups
might have changed as the values in the culture
changed. Third, these traits are attributed to
any member belonging to the category; in other
words there are no individual differences. If
a person's skin color is white, but he is
identified as black we expect all stereotyped
traits of blacks to be attributed to him.
Secord et al. (1956) provide data to show that
once a person is identified as belonging to a
category, then all traits that go with that
category are attributed to him.

    In a study using Asch's central traits para-
digm, Haire and Grunes (1950) found stereotyping and perceptual defenses at work in organizational contexts. They had provided their
subjects with two almost identical lists of
attributes describing a factory worker. The
main difference was that in one list an additional bit of information, that the worker
went to union meetings, was included. One of
the attributes contained in each list was intelligent. Respondents had difficulty reacting
to the worker who was intelligent. Apparently,
this attribute was not part of the factory
worker stereotype. Further lists deleted that
trait. The study showed also that perceptual
defenses were at work as some subjects denied
the worker was intelligent. Others distorted
or modified the information to take intelligence into account.

    Obviously, we would always expect that a
discrepancy exists between the traits that a
person attributes to a group member he has

stereotyped and the actual traits of the
group member. It should be emphasized that
stereotyping takes place because there is
actually no other information about the person
but his category. Organization members,
through daily interactions with people of
different groups, come to realize the actual
traits they possess. It is easy for them not
to stereotype, especially if they do not have
prejudicial attitudes. To eliminate prejudice
requires that people change their attitudes.
Through numerous interactions with those for
whom they hold prejudice, that may become
possible. First impressions change, as do
stereotypes, when people give them a chance.

THE ORGANIZATIONAL CONTEXT IN PERCEPTION

An organization can be likened to a culture.
It is man-made, and has a material and nonmaterial environment. The norms and values it
has evolved bring about normative behavior
from members of the organization. An organization has subgroups, much like a culture has
ethnic diversity. The perceptions of the members of an organization, in turn, can be influenced by their associational ties to certain
subgroups and by how well they have been
socialized to the organizational context. Members can be selective in their perception of
solutions to problems, depending on what are
their departmental allegiances. Dearborn and
Simon (1958) asked executives of a company
enrolled in a training program to examine a
case and indicate the problems facing an industrial organization. Nearly every one of the
executives identified the problem as belonging
to his own department. It is not important
whether the executives were right in their
judgments. What matters is that each had his
own perceptual set, and therefore saw the same
problem in a different way. Perceptual selectivity works as well in organizations as in
our everyday encounters. It would be no sur-
prise to find that we develop prejudices and

that we stereotype colleagues working in different departments. It is interesting to note that in most cases people are unwilling to change their stereotypes. They use perceptual defenses rather than give up a stereotype that, in the past, has fulfilled its economizing function. Nevertheless, organization members have to be attuned to the perceptual processes in the organization. They work and interact with people. Therefore, it is always important to be able to predict how coworkers will react in the future. Impressions of their behavior which have the stamp of constancy will help in these predictions, for these impressions constitute the base of knowledge requisite for successful future interactions.

A person's surroundings and his membership in a group exerts a strong influence on his perceptions, as explained in this chapter. But perceptions are not only influenced by external factors. Internal states also play an important part. Any behavior exhibited by a person is an effect of external stimuli and internal states such as motives, emotions, needs, and beliefs. In the following chapters we shall look in more detail at some of these internal states.

NOTES

[1] See Köhler (1947) for a statement on the Gestalt school.

[2] See Hilgard and Atkinson (1967).

REFERENCES

Anderson, N. H. "Application of an Additive Model to Impression Formation." *Science 138* (1962): 817-18.

_____. "Likableness Ratings of 555 Personality-trait Words." *Journal of Personality and Social Psychology 9* (1968a): 272-79.

_____. "Application of a Linear-serial Model to a Personality-Impression Task Using Special Presentation." *Journal of Personality and Social Psychology* 10 (1968b): 354-62.

Asch, S. E. "Forming Impressions of Personality." *Journal of Abnormal and Social Psychology* 41 (1946): 258-90.

Bruner, J. S., and Goodman, C. C. "Value and Needs as Organizing Factors in Perception." *Journal of Abnormal and Social Psychology* 42 (1947): 33-44.

Bruner, J. S., and Tagiuri, R. "Person Perception." In *Handbook of Social Psychology*, vol. 2, edited by G. Lindzey. Reading, Mass.: Addison-Wesley, 1954.

Cronbach, L. J. "Processes Affecting Scores on 'Understanding of Others' and 'Assumed Similarity'." *Psychological Bulletin* 22 (1955): 177-93.

Darwin, C. *The Expression of Emotions in Man and Animals*. London: Murray, 1872.

Dearborn, D. C., and Simon, H. A. "Selective Perception: A Note on the Departmental Identifications of Executives." *Sociometry* 21 (1958): 140-44.

Ervin-Tripp, S. "An Issei Learns English." *Journal of Social Issues* 23 (1967): 78-90.

Haire, M. "Role Perceptions in Labor Management Relations: An Experimental Approach." *Industrial and Labor Relations Review* 8 (1955): 204-16.

Haire, M., and Grunes, W. F. "Perceptual Defenses: Processes Protecting an Original Perception of Another Personality." *Human Relations* 3 (1950): 403-12.

Hastorf, A. H.; Schneider, D. J.; and Polefka, J. *Person Perception*. Reading, Mass.: Addison-Wesley, 1970.

Hilgard, E. R., and Atkinson, R. C. *Introduction to Psychology*. 4th ed. New York: Harcourt, Brace and World, 1967.

Kaplan, M. G. "Context Effects in Impression Formation: The Weighted Average Versus the Meaning-Change

Formulation." *Journal of Personality and Social Psychology 19* (1971): 92–99.

Katz, D., and Braly, K. W. "Racial Prejudice and Racial Stereotypes." *Journal of Abnormal and Social Psychology 28* (1933): 280–90.

Kelley, H. H. "The Warm–Cold Variable in the First Impressions of Persons." *Journal of Personality 18* (1950): 431–39.

Köhler, W. *Gestalt Psychology*. New York: Liveright Publishing Corp., 1947.

Levine, R.; Chein, I.; and Murphy, G. "The Relation of the Intensity of a Need to the Amount of Perceptual Distortion: A Preliminary Report." *Journal of Psychology 13* (1942): 283–93.

Lippmann, W. *Public Opinion*. Baltimore: Penguin, 1922.

Luchins, A. S. "Primacy–Recency in Impression Formation." In *The Order of Presentation in Persuasion*, edited by C. Hovland. New Haven, Conn.: Yale University Press, 1957.

McGinnies, E. "Emotionality and Perceptual Defense." *Psychological Review 56* (1949): 244–51.

Sapir, E. "Language and Environment." *American Anthropologist 14* (1912): 226–42.

Schlosberg, H. "The Description of Facial Expressions in Terms of Two Dimensions." *Journal of Experimental Psychology 44* (1952): 229–37.

Secord, P. F., and Backman, C. W. *Social Psychology*. 2nd ed. New York: McGraw–Hill, 1974.

Secord, P. F.; Bevan, W.; and Katz, B. "The Negro Stereotype and Perceptual Accentuation." *Journal of Abnormal and Social Psychology 53* (1956): 78–83.

Segall, M. H.; Campbell, D. T.; and Herskovits, M. J. *The Influence of Culture in Visual Perception*. Indianapolis: Bobbs Merrill, 1966.

Steiner, I. D. "Interpersonal Behavior as Influenced by Accuracy of Social Perception." *Psychological Review 62* (1955): 268–75.

Tajfel, H. "Social and Cultural Factors in Perception."

In *The Handbook of Social Psychology.* 2d ed. Vol.
3, edited by G. Lindzey and E. Aronson. Reading,
Mass.: Addison-Wesley, 1969, pp. 315-94.

Triandis, H. C., and Fishbein, M. "Cognitive Interaction in Person Perception." *Journal of Abnormal and
Social Psychology 67* (1963): 446-53.

Whorf, B. L. *Language, Thought, and Reality: Selected
Writings.* Edited by J. B. Caroll. Cambridge, Mass.:
Technology Press of M.I.T., 1956.

Wishner, J. "Reanalysis of 'Impressions of Personality'." *Psychological Review 67* (1960): 96-112.

3

Motivation

Motivation is a general term that refers to
processes regulating goal-directed behavior.
This process is studied in terms of what
arouses the organism to action, how behavior
is directed towards a goal, how behavior persists under the environmental conditions, and
finally how behavior is terminated.

The study of motivation has an interesting
history. In 1859, Darwin suggested that certain instinctual behaviors were crucial for
the survival of the human race. These instinctual behaviors were innate and served adaptive
functions for the organism. McDougall (1908)
was the first behavioral scientist to argue
that behavior is purposive (goal-seeking). He
posited that innate *instincts* were responsible
for purposive behavior. These instincts were
biological in nature and were viewed as unlearned predispositions to behavior. McDougall
developed the notion of a list of instincts to

explain behavior. However, this created a
problem because every time a behavior that
could not be explained by the existing list of
instincts occurred, a new instinct had to be
made up and incorporated into the all-inclu-
sive list. Later, as it became clearer that
learning theory explained how and why people
developed the behavioral characteristics they
have, the instinct viewpoint was given up.
Freud (1920), too, influenced the thinking in
motivation. He explained that frequently what
guides a person's behavior is not immediately
apparent because it may be rooted in the
unconscious. He claimed that man's unconscious
desires were responsible for purposive behavior. Modern motivation theories give the
unconscious aspect of motivation little emphasis. Yet, there is reason to believe that
unconscious motivation may play a part in guiding
behavior. This may happen because people sometimes develop habits that they are unaware of,
or because motives that are acquired under unpleasant circumstances are repressed by the
person.

Motivation is studied as a chain of events
starting from a need that is activated, con-
tinuing with a behavior that is emitted by
the organism, and ending with a reduction of
tension because the need that originally gave
rise to motivated behavior was satisfied. We
shall introduce the *drive model*, which explains
motivation within this framework. This model
traces motivation to its physiological roots
and describes well only simple behaviors. The
assumptions of the drive model will be en-
larged in the *arousal model* to incorporate motivation that does not seem to have a physiological
referent. This will allow us to explain complex
behaviors of the order of creativity and
curiosity.

Using these two models as stepping stones
we shall describe two broad theoretical approaches to the study of motivation in

organizations. First, *need-satisfaction theories*
will be described and evaluated. These theories are content oriented in that they deal
with the factors that arouse, direct, and sustain behavior. Second, we shall explain *instrumentality theories* and evaluate them. These
theories are more process oriented in that
they describe how behavior is guided. Instrumentality theorists are concerned with describing how the path that leads to a goal is
influenced by the perceptions and values of
the members of the organization. We shall
emphasize that the causes of a person's behavior cannot be explained by enumerating
factors that influence the behavior, as the
need-satisfaction theorists prefer to do. It
is only through a process explanation that we
may hope to understand the joint effects of
personal and environmental factors on behavior. Instrumentality theories emerge as an
approximative attempt to study motivation as a
process.

THE DRIVE MODEL

Motivation has generally been viewed as occurring in a cycle that starts and ends within
the organism. The *drive model* accounts for this
process by identifying physiological correlates
of motivated behavior. Motivation itself is a
hypothetical construct. One observes behavior
and also hopes to specify the physiological
arousal of the organism. The drive model explains how behavior starts and terminates and
what happens when goals toward which behavior
is directed are blocked.

HOMEOSTASIS

Homeostasis can be defined as a tendency
towards consistency. In biology the term is
used to suggest that the body has a need to
maintain a constant condition. The concept
denotes that at physiological levels,

individuals try to maintain steady states, and a balanced organism. In its classicial formulation the mechanisms (behaviors) used to restore homeostasis will depend on previous experiences. This ideal level of balance changes only to the extent that one's experiences are constantly incorporated into the process of formulating the behavior that satisfies the motivated state.

A person's motivation depends first on the strength of his existing needs. A *need* is defined as a state that involves any lack or deficit within the organism. If the need is strong and prepotent (that is, the one that has the highest influence) among all the organism's needs, it will lead to tension or a *drive* that energizes the organism to fulfill the need. A need suggests a deficiency in the organism, whereas a drive suggests that the need is strong enough to direct energy towards its fulfillment. Many authors have used the word *motive* to refer to a drive. The drive stimulates a search in the behavior repertoire of the organism for the appropriate behavior that will satisfy the attainment of the goal, thus fulfilling the need that started the process. This circular approach is very much in line with the idea of homeostasis, suggesting that need satisfaction restores balance (see Figure 3.1). For example, hunger is a need. It will generate tension and motivate a person to consume food. The search for and consummation of food, mediated by internal states of the organism, such as needs, is the subject matter of motivated behavior. The satisfaction of hunger and restoration of the organsim to its previous level is the tendency towards homeostasis.

The concept of drive is very important to the understanding of motivation. The student of motivation tries to explain how the organism is activated, energized, and aroused, and the direction of the behavior that takes place. As we have explained, a drive results from a need; the biological need arises because of a

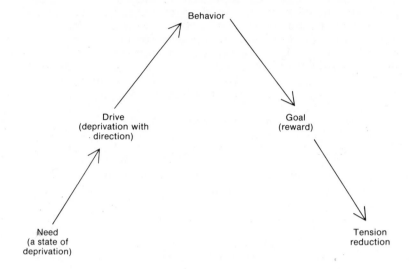

FIGURE 3.1 The motivation sequence.

state of deprivation. Therefore, a drive is a
state of deprivation with direction. It is the
cue that goads the organism into activity.
How does a drive lead to goal-directed behavior? Hull (1943) is credited for the systematic investigation of this subject. He suggested that a drive can be followed by either
an unlearned or learned behavior sequence. The
learned behavior sequence, which he called a
habit, was visualized as a stimulus-response
sequence. Thus a hunger drive would, for example, lead you to a cafeteria, as you have
learned that it is the place that will reduce
your heightened state of stimulation. In later
reformulations, Hull (1952) and his student
Spence (1956) posited that motivated behavior
was not only a result of drive and habit but
also of the incentive available in the environment to activate the habit (that is, the
amount of reward and whether one expects to
get the reward).

The drive state leads to several types of behaviors that will obtain a goal, thus resulting
in the reduction of tension in the organism
that satisfies the drive state. Kimble and
Garmezy (1968) suggest the following to be the
most important types of motivated behavior:

1. *Consummatory behavior*. This type of behavior
   directly satisfies the need that has been
   aroused. For example, eating at the cafeteria will satisfy the hunger need.
2. *Instrumental behavior*. This type of behavior is
   instrumental in satisfying the need that has
   been aroused. Walking to the cafeteria
   after class ends is instrumental in obtaining food. However, this type of behavior
   does not directly satisfy the hunger need,
   as consummatory behavior does.

GOAL BLOCKAGE AND FRUSTRATION

Once deprivation leads to a drive and the
organism identifies the appropriate goal behavior, what happens if the goal toward which
the organism is striving is blocked? For example, as you enter the cafeteria to fill
your tray, you discover that you do not have
any money to pay for it. A barrier is set between your goal-directed behavior and the goal
itself, and we refer to this situation as *goal
blockage*. This situation is usually defined as
a frustrating one. *Frustration* itself can be conceived as a motivational state that produces
tension in the organism. The tension generated
by the arousal of hunger now has shifted to
finding the funds to pay for food. Remaining
within the homeostatic model, one would have
to posit that frustration would lead to a
search for behaviors that have the end result
of reducing frustration. Early theorists suggested that frustration led to aggressive behavior, positing what has come to be known as
the *frustration-aggression hypothesis* (Dollard et
al., 1939). Frustration as a motivational force

has been studied extensively, and the initial
hypothesis has been elaborated to maintain
that aggression is not the sole response to
frustration. It is important to keep in mind
that the concept of frustration can be very
useful in understanding why sometimes an ongoing motivational sequence does not produce
the predicted behavior. Perhaps the reason why
an individual does not try to obtain certain
organizational rewards is not that he lacks
motivation, but that barriers unforeseen by the
supervisor intervene between the individual's
efforts and the organizational goals, frustrating the person. In this sense strikes and
aggression toward supervisors can be seen as
responses triggered by frustration over desirable but unattainable goals.

PRIMARY AND SECONDARY MOTIVES

All motives are not physiologically based.
Psychologists make a distinction between
physiologically based unlearned motives, called
primary motives, and those motives that are
learned, called *secondary motives*. Hunger, thirst,
sex-drive, pain, and fatigue are primary motives, but they would not be extremely useful
in explaining organizational behavior. The
study of these motives and their behavioral
consequences has dominated the field of motivation research, perhaps because the consequent
behaviors were more objectively agreed on, and because animals could as easily be used as subjects as human beings in the research.

As the individual grows in complexity the
primary drives give rise to learned secondary
drives. These drives are learned because they
excite the organism towards activities whose
reinforcement value is known. That is, secondary motives come to be learned through their
reinforcement bonds. Achievement, affiliation,
and power are examples of secondary motives.

THE AROUSAL MODEL

The fact that some behaviors originate without an apparent need for tension reduction has led to enlarging the assumptions of the drive model. We shall explain competence motivation as such an example.

COMPETENCE MOTIVATION

The drive model accounts for motivation by positing that tension reduction is the desirable end state. Also in its classical form the model suggests that there will be a physiological correlate for all basic motives. Young organisms exhibit basic motives such as hunger or pain which have physiological tendencies, but they also exhibit activity, investigation and manipulation of the environment. The physiological correlates are difficult to specify for those motives. For example, curiosity does not necessarily require tension reduction in the organism. Take the case of a person who is satiated with food. Curiosity can propell him to try new foods after all physiological tensions are reduced in his organism.

These various motives that have no physiological correlates are part of the makeup of the organism which help it to function effectively. They allow the organism to meet the challenge created by the environment. This motivational search for effective functioning has been called *competence motivation* by White (1959). Competence motivation develops early in life. Children start exploring their environments; they pull their toys apart and put them back together. This striving for competence is tied to the concept of expectancy which we will discuss in the next section. Briefly, it states that the past successes and failures of the person will influence his feelings of competence. White suggests that in adults the motivation for competence energizes behavior aimed at mastery of one's occupation. The environment provides the challenge which the individual meets with his skills, abilities, and efforts. This suggests that boring, routine jobs where the environment provides no challenge may not provide an individual with the opportunity to exercise his need for competence.

SEARCH FOR AROUSAL

Suggestions that organisms at times seek increased and at other times reduced stimulation, and that behavior persists in instances not characterized by need deprivation, have led to a reformulation of the homeostatic approach, known as *activation-arousal theory*. This view suggests that the stimulus has an impact on the arousal level of the organism, and at any given time there is an optimum arousal level which the individual strives to maintain. This is still a balance or equilibrium approach, since it postulates a tendency to maintain an optimum level of arousal. However, the stimulus, through its meaningfulness, complexity, and frequency of past occurrences, will influence the level of arousal. This position is similar to White's postulate that reduced stimulation is not always a desired state.[1]

MOTIVATION APPLIED TO ORGANIZATIONAL BEHAVIOR

Various theories have been developed in the last three decades to explain motivation at the job. Although these theories have the common goal of describing what guides behavior in organizational settings, each is different in what it chooses to investigate and explain. The theories can be divided into two groups: 1) need-satisfaction theories, and 2) instrumentality theories.

Need-satisfaction theories are concerned with the identification of specific unsatisfied needs. They propose to study the individual and particularly his environment to see what initiates, sustains, and extinguishes behavior, whereas *instrumentality theories* try to explain the process by which behavior is directed toward specific goals. Crucial variables in these theories are the identification and understanding of the antecedent conditions of action and the instrumental behaviors requisite for satisfactory goal attainment.

NEED-SATISFACTION THEORIES

There are two important need-satisfaction theories. We shall briefly discuss the major assumptions of *Maslow's hierarchical theory* and *Herzberg's two-factor theory* and then evaluate and criticize them.

MASLOW'S HIERARCHICAL THEORY. The motivational theory that has enjoyed the most success among those interested in organizational behavior has been one that was written from a humanistic viewpoint and not necessarily to explain work motivation. Maslow's (1954) explanation of motivation can be summarized in two propositions:

1. Needs are ordered along a hierarchy that begins with those important for biological survival. There are five levels in Maslow's proposed *need hierarchy*. The physiological needs are followed by needs for safety, love, esteem, and self-actualization, in that order.
2. The prepotent need level in the hierarchy will guide behavior. The person satisfies each level in the need hierarchy in order. Biological needs such as hunger, thirst, and sex guide the organism to action, and activate relevant behaviors when they have not been satisfied. Their satisfaction makes higher level needs prepotent in the hierarchy. A need that is satisfied will not motivate the organism. One would have to go one level up in the need hierarchy

to find the cause that motivates the organism.

These ideas appealed to organizational theorists because they could use them to explain historical developments related to workers. Late in the nineteenth century, workers started criticizing their working conditions for being dehumanizing. Maslow's theory had posited that man's essential survival needs are of a physiological and security nature. From the onset of the industrial movement, factories, by offering work, met these first-level needs. Once the worker began to have food on the table and shelter for his family, he became aware that the assembly line did not provide the satisfaction of the higher level needs, such as esteem. Such problems as boredom and job meaninglessness could now be remedied (if one followed Maslow's approach) by meeting the higher order needs. Studies testing Maslow's conceptualization have unfortunately failed to support the theory.[2]

HERZBERG'S TWO-FACTOR THEORY. Herzberg, Mausner, and Snyderman (1959) tried to apply Maslow's theoretical framework to the work situation. Later, based on a study he conducted with two hundred accountants and engineers, Herzberg (1966) proposed a two-factor theory of job motivation. His approach can also be explained by two propositions:

1. There are certain job-related factors that can reduce dissatisfaction with the job. These *hygiene factors*, as Herzberg called them, cannot motivate the individual. They prevent dissatisfaction. When pay is low, for example, persons become dissatisfied. But Herzberg and others argue that when pay is increased, satisfaction does not increase. Factors such as company policies, salary, supervision, interpersonal relations at the work place, and working conditions were termed hygiene factors.

2. There is a second set of factors called *motivators*. Their presence leads to satisfaction of the employee, but their absence does not arouse dissatisfaction. Factors that have motivational powers include achievement, recognition, the work itself, responsibility, and advancement.

EVALUATION AND CRITICISM OF NEED-SATISFACTION THEORIES. The influence of Maslow's theory on Herzberg's work is immediately apparent. The hygiene factors correspond to the physiological and safety needs in Maslow's "need hierarchy" explanation of human motivation. The motivators are closely related to the higher-order needs. It can be argued that Herzberg tries to apply Maslow's principles of human motivation to a specific instance, job motivation.

Need-satisfaction theories have provided conceptually interesting explanations of behavior in the work place. But theories and the data have not fit together well, the theories not being well enough constructed to guide empirical research. Both theories suffer from problems of definition and prediction. For example, it has been very difficult to operationalize and measure Maslow's highest need, that of *self-actualization*, often defined as seeking self-fulfillment or becoming a unique individual. Both models have also been criticized as being insufficiently dynamic. Each derives from homeostatic notions. The tension reduction idea is present in both Maslow's and Herzberg's theories in the sense that needs arouse and direct the organism to action. Their satisfaction brings the organism to a steady state, albeit temporarily, until a new need in the hierarchy, as yet unsatisfied, becomes prepotent. It must be emphasized that the movement of the individual along a continuum of needs, with higher needs waiting in turn to be satisfied after the lower needs, is a parsimonious (that is, simple) explanation of human behavior. If two theories can explain the same phenomena, the more parsimonious one is

preferred, and *parsimony* with high explicative
powers is a desirable tenet that any theory
should hope to incorporate.

Research on Maslow's and Herzberg's theories
of motivation has produced findings in disagreement with their basic postulates. In
Herzberg's case the problem has been that there
is no clear-cut distinction between the hygiene
and motivator factors. Herzberg arrived at his
classification through the data he collected.
In a sense, the factor categories were empirically derived. However, it has been found that
what is a motivator in one organization can be
a hygiene factor in a different organization
(King, 1970). House and Wigdor (1967) claim
that their research into data presented by
Herzberg leads them to conclude that satisfiers
and dissatisfiers are not unidimensional and
independent of each other. This may suggest
that not only does the need state of the individual have to be understood, but that the
situational characteristics have as well to be
emphasized. Also, there is reason to believe
that the differences between the factors that
bring about satisfaction and dissatisfaction
may have been a result of flaws in the data
collection, wherein the respondents had a
chance to react to the questions in a defensive
manner (Vroom, 1964).

INSTRUMENTALITY THEORIES

Maslow's and Herzberg's theories addressed
themselves to the question of arousal of the
organism. They were trying to explain how behavior starts, proceeds, and ends; what conditions instigate the organism to start an
activity, to maintain, and to terminate it.
Given their explanations, there still remains
the question of directionality of behavior.
The question of what form the activity will
take, that is, what choices among alternative
goal-satisfying responses the organism will
select, has also interested motivation theorists. Various writers have tried to explain

theoretically the choice of activity made by individuals from a repertoire of available voluntary responses. These writings have been influenced heavily by the doctrine of philosophical hedonism which states that individuals behave in such a way as to maximize certain outcomes (such as rewards, satisfactions) and to minimize other outcomes (such as punishment). Motivational theories that try to explain how behavioral choices are made are called *instrumentality theories*. The common point in all the theories is the hypothesis that behavior is partially determined by: a) the person's expectation that his behavior will lead to various outcomes, and b) the person's evaluation of these outcomes (Mitchell and Biglan, 1971). These considerations appear also in decision making and some attitude theories, as we shall see in the next two chapters. Table 3.1 lists these theories and summarizes their major constructs.[3]

VROOM'S EXPECTANCY THEORY. *Vroom's* (1964) *expectancy theory* is based on two major motivational constructs, those of *expectancy* and *value*. Vroom assumes that when people choose from alternative courses of action, these choices are lawfully related to contemporaneous psychological events. Using a multiplicative model, Vroom suggests that the expectancy of achieving a desired outcome times the value of the desired outcome (which he calls valence) results in a force akin to motivation.

Valence and *expectation* are two terms that need to be explained in his model:

VALENCE: This basically refers to the preference a person has for a certain outcome. The assumption is that at any time a person has preferences among existing states of nature. In the simple case, where there are two alternatives, say low (X_1) and high (X_2) performance, the person can prefer X_1 to X_2, X_2 to X_1 or be indifferent. The behavioral sciences use different terms to refer to preference. Valence, incentive, expected utility, attitude,

TABLE 3.1 Important variables in instrumentality theories.

Theorist	Major motivational constructs		Resultant
Vroom (1964)	Expectancy of achieving de- sired outcome	x Value of → desired outcome (valence)	Force
Porter & Lawler (1968)	Probability of achieving de- sired reward through effort	x Value of → reward	Effort
House (1971)	Path instru- mentality of achieving goal through be- havior	x Value of → reward	Motiva- tion

need, value, interest have all been used at one time or another to connote preference. Valence in this model is not synonymous with value of an outcome, which denotes satisfaction obtained when an outcome is achieved; rather, valence suggests the anticipated satisfaction that an outcome may bring about. Valence is positive for an individual when he wants to obtain a given outcome and negative when he does not. Indifference to the outcome results in zero valence.

An activity such as performance may acquire a positive valence, that is, performance as a means may be desired by an individual because it may be perceived to lead to promotion, that is, to a desirable outcome. Of course the same first-level outcome, performance, may lead to a variety of second-level outcomes, such as promotion, better interpersonal relations with supervisors, increased wages, and so on. Here a distinction is made between *first-level outcomes* and *second-level outcomes*. The former can be conceptualized as the means that lead to the latter, the ends. The perception of this functional relationship between first- and second-level outcomes is called *instrumentality*. The value of the instrumentality relationship varies between -1 and +1. If a first-level outcome is never perceived as leading to attaining a particular second-level outcome, the instrumentality relationship is -1, and if the first-level outcome is perceived as always leading to the attainment of a particular second-level outcome then the instrumentality relationship is +1.

The valence of an outcome is defined by Vroom as a monotonically increasing function of the algebraic sum of the product of the valences of all other outcomes and the person's conceptions of the specific outcome's instrumentality for the attainment of these other outcomes.

Symbolically: $V_j = f \sum_{k=1}^{n} (V_k I_{jk})$

Where:

V_j = the valence of outcome j;

I_{jk} = the perceived instrumentality of outcome j for the attainment of outcome k;

V_k = valence of outcome k;

and, n = the number of outcomes.

EXPECTATION: The other major motivational construct is that of expectancy. *Expectancy* is defined as the probability that effort will bring about a first-level outcome. It is the probability (ranging from 0 to 1) that a line of action can bring about a specific first-level outcome. If high performance is the desired first-level outcome, then expectancy refers to the probability that expending more effort will be perceived as leading to higher performance. Expectancy, then, associates actions and outcomes, and instrumentality associates outcomes to outcomes.

Valences and expectancies combine in Vroom's model to determine how a choice of action is made. The concept that guides directionality of behavior is called *force*. Force is the sum of the values of all the outcomes times the expectancies that the act will be followed by the attainment of these outcomes (that is, $F = \Sigma VE$).

To measure motivation by using Vroom's approach we would have to measure valence, instrumentality, and expectancy. We could list a number of second-level outcomes such as an increase in salary, job security, increased responsibility, promotion, and so on, and ask workers to rank their importance (see Figure 3.2). This ranking would constitute the valence scores. Then we would ask the workers whether the likelihood that increasing their performance (first-level outcome) would lead to the second-level outcomes. For example, we could say: "An increase in my performance will lead to an increase in my salary," and ask that this statement be rated on a scale going from very likely to very unlikely. A number of such statements, each linking the first-level outcome to the different second-level outcomes, would constitute the instrumentality score. Finally, the worker is asked to assess the probability that if he expends effort, higher performance would result. By substituting the obtained scores in the formulas, one can arrive at the strength of the force acting on the worker to increase his performance.[4]

HOUSE'S PATH-GOAL THEORY. House (1971) has proposed a theory where the leader is seen as clarifying the paths to the organizational and

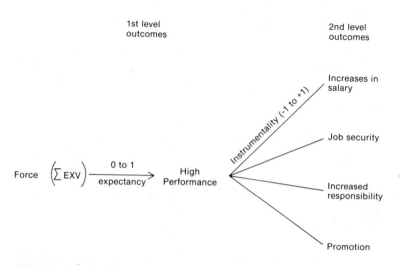

FIGURE 3.2 A diagrammatic representation of the variables in Vroom's (1964) model.

personal goals of his subordinates. The theory predicts that by performing motivating functions, the leader can influence the variables entering into the subordinate's motivation equation, thereby increasing the subordinate's performance and satisfaction.

The variables of expectation and value, which are at the core of every instrumentality theory, have been broken down to their component parts in House's approach. He sees work motivation as resulting from intrinsic and extrinsic valences associated with outcomes (which he calls work-goals) and the probability (which he calls path instrumentality) that behavior leads to goal attainment. Motivation is viewed as a result of external and internal forces. Instrumentality, to an extent, depends on external agents (for example, supervisors) recognizing the person's success in accomplishing the goal and rewarding him accordingly. But, if the behavior has intrinsic valence, then it is intrinsically motivating too,

because the behavior becomes instrumental for
goal satisfaction. If the valence is extrinsic,
the behavior may or may not be motivating. The
theory explains the path to the attainment of
the goal, and describes some of the processes
along the path.[5] Further, the theory postulates
how the leader can perform motivating functions.

PORTER'S AND LAWLER'S PERFORMANCE THEORY.
Porter and Lawler (1968) have suggested a more
complete model of motivation. Their model dif-
fers from Vroom's and House's in that they include more contingencies to describe the final
behavior and they look at performance rather
than valence. Figure 3.3 depicts the Porter
and Lawler model of work motivation.

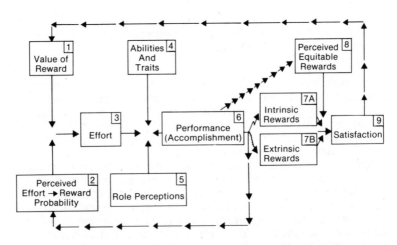

SOURCE: L. W. Porter and E. E. Lawler, III (1968),
p. 165.

FIGURE 3.3 The Porter and Lawler performance model.

The key variable in the model is effort. In
this case, effort means motivation, not performance. Effort is determined by the value
that a reward has for an individual and the

the situation. The reward or incentive puts him under the control of the source of reward. The loss of control does not have desirable motivational consequences. It can result in reduction of task motivation rather than enhancement of it. Whether this effect generalizes from a laboratory situation to work situations has yet to be shown.

Perhaps Herzberg's theory on the various factors that affect the satisfaction dimension best expressed the idea that satisfaction is multidimensional. This makes the measurement of satisfaction difficult. Somehow, one usually expects a fit between performance and satisfaction. Brayfield and Crockett (1955) have shown the nonexistence of this expected fit. Schwab and Cummings (1970) suggest that a reason for the lack of reliable findings on satisfaction and performance is that satisfaction has been poorly defined. It is sometimes used in the "narrow" need deprivation connotation, and at other times in a "broad" attitudinal sense. They also posit that there may be potential moderator variables that relate performance and satisfaction. One such moderator variable is occupational or job level. Even though most instrumentality models examined so far have posited that performance causes satisfaction when this relationship is perceived as such by the subject, the evidence has not been experimental.

One moderator variable that may influence effort, performance, and/or satisfaction is the presence of others in the situation. Groups compel individuals to adopt certain behaviors. It has been shown that groups may facilitate the expression of motivated behavior. If we wanted to understand motivation as a process, we would have to understand what influences the person to select a given path toward the goal. Other people, simply by their presence, may influence an individual's performance (Zajonc, 1965). Kiesler (1978) elaborates on the importance of interpersonal processes on behavior.

An Important Secondary Motive: Achievement

Western societies have often been described as "achieving" societies. Philosophers and historians, novelists and psychologists have described the Western world as stressing the values of accomplishment, success, and competition. Even though these values have been used to describe cultures and explain their accomplishments in general, at the level of the individual, psychologists have been confronted with the problem in specific terms: Why is it that certain people succeed better at what they are doing than others? Why do some workers and managers accomplish more than others holding similar jobs at similar levels of authority in the same culture and across cultures? Besides economic, technological, and situational factors specific to certain organizations, are there any factors inherently individual that explain why some people succeed and others do not? We shall look to studies in achievement motivation to find some of the answers.

McClelland's Work on Achievement Motivation

McClelland's (1961) work on achievement motivation is an attempt to answer these questions. He suggested that achievement in itself may be an important intrinsically motivational force. He further suggested that a person's past experiences will determine the extent to which he will develop achievement motivation more than another person not subject to the same past experiences. The advantages of such a theoretical formulation are that they allow for: 1) operationalization of an achievement motive; 2) a specification of those individuals that would develop it; 3) a possibility of predicting those who would behave in an achievement-oriented fashion in certain situations.

Achievement motivation is measured by a projective test. In such a test the person is confronted with an ambiguous stimulus (such as an ink blot or a picture) and asked to verbalize what he perceives. The technique allows for inner feelings and motives to be projected on the test (see Figure 3.4). McClelland showed that it was possible to manipulate the level of achievement-motivation by giving subjects different instructions. When subjects are told that they are being measured against criteria of excellence, their stories tend to include more achievement-related content than when they are given neutral instructions. The next logical step is to demonstrate that people who score high on achievement imagery in thought samples exhibit different behaviors than those who score low. This is the search for validity of the construct. Various experiments have shown that the projective test used (called the Thematic Apperception Test or TAT) can predict differential behavior in a situation. The most replicated and well-known finding was that people with high achievement motivation tended to be moderate risk-takers (Atkinson and Litwin, 1960).

McClelland has also tried to explain economic growth via a psychological construct, such as achivment motivation. He postulated that certain religious and cultural values lead parents to instill independence and mastery in their children. Winterbottom (1958) had found that boys who demonstrated high need achievement (*n-Ach*) had mothers who wanted their sons to be independent and master their environment at an earlier age than boys who scored low on *n-Ach*. McClelland reasoned that if parents in a culture stressed achievement, mastery, and self-reliance, this would affect those children that later became entrepreneurs and explain the economic growth of that culture. He tested

FIGURE 3.4 A TAT picture used to measure achievement.
The person is asked to look at the picture briefly and
then to write out the story the picture suggests.

his thesis in ingenious ways to show that
countries that were economically well-off in
1950 had stressed achievement twenty-five years
prior to that time. The time lag was to give a
generation the chance to become entrepreneurs.[7]

DESCRIPTION OF MANAGERS WHO HAVE HIGH ACHIEVEMENT MOTIVATION

McClelland and his students investigated
n-Ach as it influences the behaviors of managers

in various countries. The research resulted
in explaining what the characteristics of the
entrepreneurial role were, thus clarifying
the makeup of one of the major variables in
the model. The findings can be summarized
under a few propositions:

MODERATE LEVEL OF RISK TAKING: Individuals with
high n-Ach prefer situations with a moderate
level of risk. Success in a high-risk choice
may be attributable to luck, and in a low-risk
choice to not having tried. This proposition
has been corroborated by various researchers.
In the best known experiment, Atkinson and
Litwin (1960), after obtaining n-Ach scores from
their subjects, had them play a ringtoss game
where the subjects chose the distance to toss
the rings. Those with high n-Ach always chose
the moderate distance from the peg.

ACCEPTANCE OF PERSONAL RESPONSIBILITY FOR DE-
CISIONS AND RESULTS OF WORK: The person with
high n-Ach prefers to be credited with the success of his own work.

BEING MORE ENERGETIC: High n-Ach individuals
will work harder only if they know that the
task brings personal achievement or that their
personal efforts will influence the outcome.

TAKING MORE RESPONSIBILITY FOR INITIATING
DECISIONS: This seems to satisfy managers even
more than recognition received for individual
accomplishment.

FEEDBACK CONCERNING THE SUCCESS OR FAILURE OF
DECISIONS: The individual with high n-Ach will
want to know how well he has done in work situations. This facilitates the subsequent performance of the individual.

There has been tremendous output of research
on McClelland's ideas. As a motive, n-Ach, perhaps, has been the most studied, best document-
ed psychological construct. Even though all

research efforts have not been conclusive, and
all predictions from the theory not borne out,
the major tenets have survived. It can be said
with confidence that *n-Ach* correlates highly
with successful managerial behavior, even if
it is not necessarily predictive of it, as
McClelland tried to show.

ATKINSON'S EXPECTANCY MODEL OF ACHIEVEMENT MOTIVATION

Atkinson (1964) developed an instrumentality
theory approach to explain behavior specifically in achievement-oriented situations. In this
model, motivation is a multiplicative result
of expectancy, value, and strength of motive.
Thus, if we look at behavior related to
achievement in a given situation, it can be
seen as a result of: 1) the motivational disposition of the individual related to seeking
success which is assumed to be stable and is
measured by a projective test such as the TAT;
2) the person's estimate of probability of
success at the task; and 3) the incentive value
that success at the task holds for the person.
This is symbolized in Figure 3.5.

			INCENTIVE
MOTIVE	MOTIVATIONAL	EXPECTATION	VALUE OF
AROUSAL =	DISPOSITION x	OF SUCCESS x	SUCCESS
(or *n-Ach*	(Score on		
oriented	*n-Ach*)	(*P*)	(1-*P*)
behavior)			

FIGURE 3.5 Atkinson's model of achievement motivation.

The last two variables in this equation are
closely related in Atkinson's model. The assumption is that there is an inverse relationship between incentive value and probability of
success. If a person is confronted with a task
that is not very challenging, where success
may come easily, then the situation is not very
valued. Recognition for an easy task is not

highly regarded. A person will obtain more
satisfaction and pleasure by being successful
at a difficult task. But even though a difficult task has high incentive value, the
probability of success in it is low. So people
who have high motivational dispositions will
seek task situations of intermediate difficulty. This formulation is derivable mathematically from Atkinson's presentation.

AFFILIATION AND POWER AS SECONDARY MOTIVES

McClelland (1961) has looked not only at
achievement but also at affiliation and power
as important needs. The research suggests that,
generally, people high in achievement motivation are low on the need to affiliate (*n-Aff*).
This is also posited as a cultural or national
tendency. McClelland finds that when a country
is high in achievement it is low in affiliation. Managers from the United States who had
high *n-Ach* scores were found to have significantly lower *n-Aff* scores. Even though *n-Ach*
seems to push the manager to requisite entre-
preneurlike behaviors, being low in *n-Aff* may
create some problems. It suggests a disinterest
in warm and close relationships. A concern for
people is suggested as a key variable in explaining successful managerial behavior by organizational development experts. Whether high
n-Aff will actually help the manager in the work
situation is as yet a moot question, as there
are no empirical tests of the issue.
The motivation for power can be important
when considering achievement. If we describe
the success of an executive solely as a result
of a need to achieve, we may miss an important
variable, that of the need for power. It is
well accepted that a position in an organization has an explicit or implicit power refer-
rent. Thus, it is important to try to distinguish independently between achievement and
power, both of which generate affect states.
Success at a task does not necessarily imply
power, but because success may also bring

power, it may be difficult to separate the two variables. Philosophers such as Machiavelli, Hobbes, and Nietzche were very emphatic on the importance of power as one of man's important preoccupations and the vehicle for leadership. Power has not been extensively studied as a motive. The results reported by McClelland point to methodological problems of measurement. He suggests that managers score high on a measure of n-power defined as the need to influence other people.[8]

NOTES

[1]See Berlyne (1960) for a statement on activation-arousal theory.

[2]See Hall and Nougaim (1968) for a comprehensive survey.

[3]Simmons (1978) also looks at instrumentality theories from an applied viewpoint (see chapter 4).

[4]See Galbraith and Cummings (1967) and Graen (1969) for tests of Vroom's theory.

[5]See Georgopoulos, Mahoney and Jones (1957) for an initial version of the path-goal hypothesis.

[6]For a more recent statement on equity theory see Walster, Berscheid, and Walster (1973).

[7]McClelland's (1961) book includes numerous examples of how achievement was measured in this study. Also, it contains information on how the theoretical relationship was validated for countries that showed economic growth in the past such as Ancient Greece and preIncan Peru.

[8]See Swingle (1976) for a statement on the relationship between power and management.

REFERENCES

Adams, J. S. "Inequity in Social Exchange." In *Advances in Experimental Social Psychology*, vol. 2, edited by L. Berkowitz. New York: Academic Press, 1965.

Atkinson, J. W. *An Introduction to Motivation*. Princeton, N.J.: Van Nostrand, 1964.

Atkinson, J. W., and Litwin, G. H. "Achievement Motive and Test Anxiety Conceived of as a Motive to Approach Success and to Avoid Failure." *Journal of Abnormal and Social Psychology 60* (1960): 52-63.

Berlyne, D. *Conflict, Arousal and Curiosity*. New York: McGraw-Hill, 1960.

Brayfield, A. H., and Crockett, W. H. "Employee Attitudes and Employee Performance." *Psychological Bulletin 52* (1955): 394-424.

Darwin, C. *Origin of Species*. 1936 ed. New York: Modern Library, 1859.

deCharms, R. *Personal Causation*. New York: Academic Press, 1968.

Deci, E. L. "Effects of Externally Mediated Rewards on Intrinsic Motivation." *Journal of Personality and Social Psychology 18* (1971): 105-15.

_____. "Intrinsic Motivation, Extrinsic Reinforcement, and Inequity." *Journal of Personality and Social Psychology 22* (1972): 113-20.

Dollard, J.; Doob, L.; Miller, N.; Mowrer, O.; and Sears, R. *Frustration and Aggression*. New Haven: Yale Univ. Press, 1939.

Freud, S. *A General Introduction to Psychoanalysis*. New York: Liveright Publishing Corp., 1920.

Galbraith, J., and Cummings, L. L. "An Empirical Investigation of the Motivational Determinants of Task Performance: Interactive Effects Between Instrumentality-valence and Motivation-ability." *Organizational Behavior and Human Performance 2* (1967): 237-57.

Georgopoulos, B. S.; Mahoney, G. M.; and Jones, N. W. "A Path-Goal Approach to Productivity." *Journal of Applied Psychology 41* (1957): 345-53.

Graen, G. "Instrumentality Theory of Work Motivation: Some Experimental Results and Suggested Modifications." *Journal of Applied Psychology Monograph 53* (1969): 1-25.

Hall, D. T., and Nougaim, K. E. "An Examination of Maslow's Need Hierarchy in an Organizational Setting. *Organizational Behavior and Human Performance 5* (1968): 12-35.

Herzberg, F. *Work and the Nature of Man.* Cleveland: World Publishing Company, 1966.

Herzberg, F.; Mausner, B.; and Snyderman, B. *The Motivation to Work.* New York: Wiley, 1959.

House, R. J. "A Path Goal Theory of Leader Effectiveness." *Administrative Science Quarterly 16* (1971): 321-38.

House, R. J., and Wigdor, L. "Herzberg's Dual-factor Theory of Job Satisfaction and Motivation: A Review of the Evidence and Criticism." *Personnel Psychology 20* (1967): 369-89.

Hull, C. L. *Principles of Behavior.* New York: Appleton-Century-Crofts, Inc., 1943.

_____. *A Behavior System.* New Haven: Yale University Press, 1952.

Kiesler, S. B. *Interpersonal Processes in Groups and Organizations.* Arlington Heights, Ill.: AHM Publishing Corporation, 1978.

Kimble, G. A., and Garmezy, N. *General Psychology.* 3rd ed. New York: Ronald Press Co., 1968.

King, N. "Clarification and Evaluation of the Two-factor Theory of Job Satisfaction." *Psychological Bulletin 74* (1970): 18-31.

Maslow, A. H. *Motivation and Personality.* New York: Harper, 1954.

McClelland, D. C. *The Achieving Society.* Princeton: N.J.: Van Nostrand, 1961.

McDougall, W. *An Introduction to Social Psychology*. London: Methuen, 1908.

Mitchell, T. R., and Biglan, A. "Instrumentality Theories: Current Uses in Psychology." *Psychological Bulletin 76* (1971): 432-54.

Porter, L. W., and Lawler, E. E. *Managerial Attitudes and Performance*. Homewood, Ill.: Irwin and Dorsey, 1968.

Schwab, D. P., and Cummings, L. L. "Theories of Performance and Satisfaction: A Review." *Industrial Relations 4* (1970): 408-30.

Simmons, R. E. *Managing Behavioral Processes: Applications of Theory and Research*. Arlington Heights, Ill.: AHM Publishing Corporation, 1978.

Spence, K. W. *Behavior Theory and Conditioning*. New Haven: Yale University Press, 1956.

Swingle, P. *The Management of Power*. Hillsdale, N.J.: Erlbaum, 1976.

Vroom, V. H. *Work and Motivation*. New York: Wiley, 1964.

Walster, E.; Berscheid, E.; and Walster, G. W. "New Directions in Equity Research." *Journal of Personality and Social Psychology 25* (1973): 151-76.

White, R. W. "Motivation Reconsidered: The Concept of Competence." *Psychological Review 66* (1959): 297-333.

Winterbottom, M. R. "The Relation of Need for Achievement to Learning Experiences in Independence and Mastery." In *Motives in Fantasy, Action and Society*, edited by J. W. Atkinson. Princeton, N.J.: Van Nostrand, 1958.

Zajonc, R. B. "Social Facilitation." *Science 149* (1965): 269-74.

Individual
Decision-Making

A *decision* is a goal-directed behavior made by
the individual, in response to a certain need,
with the intention of satisfying the motive
that the need occasions. All behavior involves
at least simple decisions. For example, one
decides whether to walk to work or not. Many
decisions involve a choice between more than
two alternatives. One can walk to work, ride
a bicycle, take a bus, or drive his car. All
alternatives bring about the same goal, getting to work. The process of decision-making
becomes difficult because often the existence
of equally attractive, unattractive, or competing alternatives makes many decisions an
unpleasant exercise. One can become frustrated
while making a decision because the available
alternatives may generate conflict. Tension
is produced if we are uncertain about the
choice or if we are fearful of the consequences
of a wrong choice. The needs of the individual,

and his perception of the environment, are
important determiners of decision-making.

The decision process starts with problem
identification and ends with a choice. In
this chapter, we shall explain how the process
has traditionally been analyzed; we shall
study most explanations of how we decide when
we are uncertain about the probability of occurrence of each alternative.

Then two competing general approaches will be
discussed, describing how man makes decisions.
The traditional approach was developed by
economists and sees a person as trying to do
the best thing for himself while being aware
of all his options. The second approach is
the behavioral science view, where the person
is seen as trying to satisfice some personal
values while being partially aware of all the
options in the environment. We favor the latter
view because we believe that man possesses
limited capabilities for processing information
and hence cannot fulfill the demands made by
the economic model.

Decision-making models aim to *describe* how
people make decisions. The models describing
the decision-making process fit the data from
the actual decision to the prescriptions of
the model. Besides being descriptive, many
models also are normative. They tell us how
people ought to decide, or at least how the
theorist who evolved the model thinks people
ought to decide. Four such decision-making
models that have found recent exposure will be
discussed. Even though many of these models
use elegant mathematical formulations, the explanations that we shall give of the models
will, of necessity, be sketchy.

Decision-making is one of the most important
processes in life. When discussing organizations, Simon (1960) treats decision-making as
synonymous with managing. In so doing, he
underlines the fact that decision-making as
a process should not be reduced simply to a

choice among alternatives. Rather, this process
involves conceptualization of the problem to
be solved and the description of how that final
choice is made. Before one can describe the
process of decision-making, one must understand
the psychological variables that enter the
process. Our aim is to deal with the person as
a decision-maker.

THE DECISION PROCESS

The decision process begins with identification of a problem. The problem arises when a
sought-after goal can be obtained via alternative and sometimes competing avenues. A person
faced with investing money for some sort of return has alternative ways of satisfying this
goal. Simon (1960) suggests that problem identification leads first to intelligence activity, which involves searching the environment
for various conditions reflecting on the decision. Within the organizational context,
problem identification is followed by design
activity in which all options are analyzed.
Choice activity is the final step in the decision process where an alternative is selected. Decision theorists have tried to delineate
a systematic, step-by-step process for decision-making. This process is usually characterized as consisting of identification of the
problem, specification of goals, searching
for alternatives and evaluating them, and the
selection of an action.
   Identification of the problem produces a
motivational state that induces action. The
definition and clarification of the goals are
needed so that satisfaction can be obtained
through various actions and outcomes. The
person who is going to make an investment decision wants a return on the investment as the
outcome of his decision. This would satisfy
him. But further questions are raised. How
much satisfaction does he want, and how much
return would bring this satisfaction? This

leads to a discussion of the aspects surrounding a decision. To do this we shall explain how
decisions are categorized and how outcomes are
selected.

CERTAINTY, RISK, AND UNCERTAINTY INVOLVED IN CHOICE

The environment surrounding a decision is not
always known to the person. Often the person
is forced to make a decision with limited
information about the environmental conditions
of the decision. There are three conditions
under which decisions are made: certainty,
risk, and uncertainty. *Certainty* exists when the
outcome of alternative actions can be accurately predicted. In the certainty condition the
decision process involves a rule which maximizes the outcome of one or a combination of
variables. For example, profit could be such
an index to be maximized in an economic context. *Risk* involves a state in which the outcomes of the alternative actions can be specified and a probability assigned to the likelihood of the occurrence of each. To understand
choice under conditions of risk, we have to
know: 1) how the individual appraises the
probability of the occurrence of each outcome,
and 2) what personal values the person wants
to maximize (that is, what kind of satisfaction he wants to derive). *Uncertainty* exists
when the probability of occurrence of alternative outcomes is unknown. Under the condition
of uncertainty, outcomes of actions can be
determined, but the probability for their occurrence cannot be assigned.

Decisions can be viewed as ranging on a continuum of uncertainty. Decisions for which most
of the information is known or available are
at one end of this continuum and decisions for
which no knowledge exists are placed at the
other. In order to understand choice under uncertainty, we must make recourse to the perceptions, needs, and the belief system of the
individual. Under conditions of uncertainty,

subjective probabilities are often assigned in
ignorance to outcomes. Availability of information helps in reducing uncertainty. However, information is helpful only up to a point. Miller
(1956) has shown that human memory imposes
severe limitations on the amount of information
which humans can receive, process, and remember.

CRITERIA FOR DECISIONS

The decision process starts with problem
identification in which goals that may satisfy
the problem are specified. Then follows a
search for alternatives. The individual evalu-
ates these alternatives by using some kind of
criteria to eliminate all alternatives but one
that he hopes will lead to the desired outcome.
In order to describe and further predict how an
individual decides, we have to understand his
criteria. Rational criteria are easy to define
for decisions made under certainty. But the
notion of rationality becomes blurred when
risk, uncertainty, and personal values are considered.

In order to specify criteria for decisions,
let us describe the components of a decision.
Table 4.1 represents information available for
a decision. The environment is composed of
states of nature (s). The individual has different actions (a) he can take in respect to
the states of nature. For each pair (a_i, s_j)
that consists of an action and a state of
nature there will be an outcome. Each outcome
has a *payoff* for the person. Outcomes are preferred according to the subjective evaluation
of their payoffs. The preference for the outcome suggests the *utility* which the outcome has
for the person. In Table 4.1 the entries into
the matrix denote the utilities (u) that each
outcome has for the person.

When making decisions under uncertainty,
people use different criteria to select an
action strategy. Luce and Raiffa (1957) identify the following criteria: maximin gain or

TABLE 4.1 A payoff matrix.

Actions	States of Nature			
	S_1	S_2 .... S_j		S_n
a_1	U_{11}	U_{12} ...... U_{1j}		U_{1n}
a_2	U_{21}	U_{22} ...... U_{2j}		U_{2n}
.	.	.	.	.
.	.	.	.	.
a_i	U_{i1}	U_{i2} ...... U_{ij}		U_{in}
.	.	.	.	.
.	.	.	.	.
a_m	U_{m1}	U_{m2} ...... U_{mj}		U_{mn}

minimax loss, minimax regret, the pessimism-optimism index, and the principle of insufficient reason. Table 4.2 depicts a fictitious payoff matrix that demonstrates how the criteria are applied in the choice of an action.

A pessimistic action would be characterized by the principle of *maximin gain*. This strategy allows the person to capitalize on a choice that maximizes the minimum gain. For each action, the least desirable payoff is selected, and the final choice is the greatest least desirable payoff. In Table 4.2 that would correspond to A_1. The *minimax loss* principle results in the same strategy, but the decision maker is now concerned with losses. The person chooses that action with the payoff that minimizes the maximum loss. Again, for each action the least desirable payoff is selected, and the final choice is the greatest least desirable

TABLE 4.2 A Payoff Matrix and Calculation of Some Decision Criteria.

Actions	States of Nature S_1	S_2	S_3	S_4	Maximax	Maximin Gain	Principle of Insufficient Reason $= \dfrac{u_{i1}+u_{i2}+\ldots u_{in}}{n}$
A_1	9	3	4	6	9*	3*	$\dfrac{22}{4} = 5.5^*$
A_2	5	4	1	7	7	1	$\dfrac{17}{4} = 4.25$
A_3	4	8	2	5	8	2	$\dfrac{19}{4} = 4.75$

*Denotes the appropriate action choice for the criteria used.

payoff. In our example, A_1 would be the minimax loss strategy. This is known as conservative choice because the risk of loss is minimized, but large gains may also be prevented.

Savage (1951) points out that regret criteria can be calculated for a decision. A person may always wish that he had chosen another alternative. Regret can be measured by the difference between the actual payoff and the best payoff possible for every outcome. A regret matrix for our example is represented in Table 4.3. Savage has suggested the minimax regret choice where the maximum risk for each strategy is minimized. Accordingly by *minimax regret*, A_2 is the choice in our example.

TABLE 4.3 A Regret Matrix for Table 4.2 and Calculation of Minimax Regret.

Action	States of Nature S_1	S_2	S_3	S_4	MINIMAX REGRET
A_1	0	5	0	1	5
A_2	4	4	3	0	4*
A_3	5	0	2	2	5

*Denotes the appropriate action choice for the criteria used.

An optimistic choice would be a *maximax* strategy. This is the search for the state that has the highest payoff, strategy A_1 in our example. Hurwicz (see Luce and Raiffa, 1957) proposed a criterion where a combination of the best and the worst states is used. To establish this criterion, a pessimism-optimism index, α, whose values range between 0 and 1 is calculated.

One obtains a strategy by multiplying the best payoff for each action with α. Correspondingly, the worse payoff for each action is multiplied by $1 - \alpha$. After the payoffs are multiplied by the index, the action that yields the highest value is chosen. Table 4.4 shows how this is computed for an α of 0.6. This pessimism-optimism index is a psychological index that attaches subjective values through α and $1-\alpha$ to the payoffs.

TABLE 4.4 Calculation of Best Strategy Under a Pessimism-Optimism Index.

$$\alpha = .6 \qquad 1 - \alpha = .4$$

$$A_1 = (.6)9 + (.4)3 = 6.6*$$

$$A_2 = (.6)7 + (.4)1 = 4.6$$

$$A_3 = (.6)8 + (.4)2 = 5.6$$

---

*Denotes the appropriate action choice for the criteria used.

If a person is completely ignorant as to which state of nature will occur, he can apply the principle of *insufficient reason*. Here one assumes that the occurrence of each state of nature is equally likely. Since the probability of any state occurring is equally likely, the highest average payoff strategy is selected by adding the payoffs for each strategy and dividing them by the total states of nature. For the example we have been using this would give us strategy A_1 as shown in Table 4.2.

The use of two different criteria does not always provide identical results. Choice of any one of these criteria gives us some clues as to the attitudes and preferences of the person.

Minimax and maximin are pessimistic criteria. The person may choose them because he thinks he is unlucky, whereas a person who thinks of himself as somewhat lucky would use a more optimistic criterion, such as the pessimism-optimism index. The choice of any of the discussed criteria changes the problem from a decision under uncertainty to one under risk because the chooser shows certain preferences and a belief about the world. For instance minimax choice suggests a belief in the worst possible world. In engineering, the term used to denote this state is "fail-safe."

TYPES OF DECISIONS

Within organizations, individuals make decisions which are sometimes compatible with their personal goals but occasionally are not. Incompatibility between personal and organizational goals can bring further conflict into a decision. Most decisions made in an organization are of a routine nature. Examples of routine decisions can be seen when the personnel officer hires someone new, the first-line supervisor changes a part of the operation, the sales manager apportions territory, or the accountant makes entries into his books. Some decisions in the organization are more important and basic. Deciding on a new union contract or the manufacturing of a new line of products is of greater consequence than a routine decision. Routine decisions more often involve certainty or risk, whereas important decisions involve uncertainty.

Simon (1960) distinguishes two types of executive decisions: programmed and nonprogrammed. *Programmed decisions* are routine in nature. A procedure for handling programmed decisions exists in the organization and the problem-solving process involves referring to past experience. The solution for a programmable decision can be computed. New and unstructured decisions are called *nonprogrammed* because the problem has never arisen before.

Simon's terminology, borrowed from that used
for computers, suggests that some decisions
leave us with no guidelines (program) for a
step-by-step solution. Figure 4.1 shows examples of programmed and nonprogrammed decisions. It must be understood that decision
types are not always this clear-cut. They
range on a continuum of programmability. Most
programmable decisions are made under conditions of risk or uncertainty.

THE MAN WHO DECIDES

Decision-making is of interest not only to
behavioral scientists but also to those in
economics and political science. We hinted
that rationality cannot always be expected
when making a decision. The term rational
means different things to different people. The
person who makes decisions in economics and the
person who makes decisions in organizational
behavior are the same. However, each discipline
has developed its own model of the decision-
maker. Economists conceptualize the person who
makes decisions as a rational being who weighs
each alternative. Behavioral scientists, on
the other hand, have observed a decision-making
man who simplifies the world, distorts it in
accordance with his values, and often uses
chance phenomena such as coin-tossing or consulting an astrologer to make a decision.

ECONOMICALLY RATIONAL DECISION-MAKING

Economic models of man have their roots in
the pleasure principle submitted by the British
philosophers Jeremy Bentham and John Stuart
Mill. Their hedonistic approach postulated
that man tries to maximize pleasure and minimize pain. These ideas formed the basis for
postulates in economics as well as learning
theory in the behavioral sciences. Shubik
(1958) outlines the following premises made by
the economic model: Economic man is aware of

Types of Decisions	Decision-Making Techniques	
	Traditional	Modern
Programmed: Routine, repetitive decisions Organization develops specific processes for handling them	1. Habit 2. Clerical routine: Standard operating procedures 3. Organization structure; Common expectations A system of subgoals Well-defined informational channels	1. Operations research: Mathematical analysis Models Computer simulation 2. Electronics data processing
Nonprogrammed: One-shot, ill-structured novel, policy decisions Handled by general problem-solving processes	1. Judgment, intuition, and creativity 2. Rules of thumb 3. Selection and training of executives	Heuristic problem-solving techniques applied to: (a) training human decision makers (b) constructing heuristic computer programs

SOURCE: H. A. Simon (1960), p. 8.

FIGURE 4.1 Programmed and nonprogrammed decision-making.

all the alternatives in a given situation and
acts rationally to choose the most viable one.
Rationality is characterized by the fact that
the person can: 1) attach a utility to each
outcome and order the preferences according to
his utility, and 2) choose that alternative
which maximizes utility. This reflects a means-
ends analysis of rationality. If the appropriate means are chosen for specified ends, then a
decision is rational. The assumptions of the
economic man have proved to be impossible to
demonstrate in real life. First of all, it is
difficult to be aware of all alternatives.
Second, many times it is impossible to map
utility functions since individuals are unclear
about their own utility functions. Furthermore,
the function is not stable but subject to
change and little scientific progress exists
in mapping utilities on a cardinal scale.
Finally, individuals do not always choose the
maximum payoff alternative.

Each decision for the economically rational
man is programmable. However, we know that
there are nonprogrammable decisions and some
of the decisions of economics fall into this
category. The classic model of economic man
is a normative model which suggests how a
decision *ought* to be made. At best it would apply only to decisions made under certainty. Of
course, those who espouse economic rationality
accept that irrationality with utilities exists. People often prefer C to A when A was
preferred to B and B to C. Basic research into
individual consumer behavior shows this phenomenon very clearly. Adherents of the economic
model would argue that the fault does not lie
with the model but with the irrational individual. Churchman (1968) suggests that the rational approach, although flawless in its axioms,
does not tell us much of practical value about
rationality and its application to real behavior.

NONECONOMICALLY RATIONAL MAN
Simon (1947) criticized the rationality and

maximization aspects of the economic model of man by suggesting a model of decision-making man that matches reality. Rationality in economics implies a complete knowledge of the environment and the maximization of a value based on this information. Simon has argued cogently that, at any point in time, an individual has only limited information on the states of nature. It is impossible to know what each choice alternative may lead to in the future. In organizations we deal with men who have bounded rationality. Man has access only to a portion of objective reality and his behavior is in response to bounded rationality. Consequently, due to lack of economic rationality, what is maximized is not necessarily always that which yields highest utility, but an alternative acceptable to the person. A means-ends definition of rationality is also erroneous because ends are rarely objectively specifiable and they are often inseparable from means.

In opposition to the economic man, Simon proposes the administrative man who "satisfices" rather than maximizes. Administrative man is unable to have complete and accurate information about the environment, so he searches through available choice alternatives until he hits upon one that is "good enough." A choice is made when an alternative meets the minimum standard of satisfaction that the individual expects. This choice rarely coincides with an optimal decision, such as suggested by the model in economics. The interest is in feasible solutions that meet a minimal standard of satisfaction. Optimal solutions may not be feasible. During the search for a satisfactory alternative, the individual may realize that he is unable to find any alternative that meets his standards. He then lowers his level of aspiration, thereby lowering the minimum acceptable standard. If search shows that available alternatives are very satisfactory, the aspiration level may be raised. The whole process implies that the individual has a psychological set from which he determines subjective rationality. Simon (1959) also allows for rational decision-making models when the decision can be quantified in terms of utilities and occurrence probability of outcomes. Given this information, an ideal decision model can be built by mathematical tools, and the predictions of this normative model compared to the actual decisions of the individual.

Support for Simon's model comes from several areas of research. Perceptual biases as well as needs and motives discussed in the previous chapters relate evidence to the notion of psychological set. In perception we deal only with a model of reality which is in the eye of the beholder. In Simon's model, decisions are also taken within a construction of a simplified version of reality.

Soelberg (1966) has shown that search ends when a satisficing alternative is found. His research demonstrated that graduate students questioned on prospective job decisions stopped looking for a job ten days or more before reporting their decision. In trying to explain the unprogrammed decision process, Soelberg found that scalar utility could not be applied to represent the structure of human values, but that the decision process followed steps outlined by Simon. He further added to the approach by saying that the decision process is one of decision confirmation. An alternative becomes satisfactory during search, other choices are compared to it, and this alternative emerges as the choice when a satisfactory decision rule is constructed which rules out all other alternatives.

Myers and Fort (1963) found that level of aspiration in betting was based on the preceding pattern of outcomes. If the bettor won, another win was predicted. This agrees with the success and failure notion that characterizes level of aspiration. Success leads to raising aspirations and failures lower them. The whole notion of satisficing is rooted in motivational

tendencies. Search is geared for drive satisfaction. However, the conditions which will
satisfy a drive state are not invariant; rather, they change with the level of aspiration,
which itself is rooted in the person's experience (Lewin et al., 1944). Simon's proposition
about level of aspiration and the research
demonstrate the fallacy of economic rationality. If a person were to maximize his returns,
then the level of aspiration would have to be
absolute. If we view decision-making as goal-
directed behavior, then our concern is with
the reduction of tension that develops prior
to making the decision. Psychological theory
shows that this is done by choosing a satisficing alternative.

Administrative people operate on a simplified
version of the real world. This is due to the
information available on the one hand, and
their capability to process information on the
other hand. Complex models built by operations
research can aid organization people in making
decisions. But limits to information processing
lead many individuals to simplify the models.
Hirschman and Lindblom (1962) suggest that the
decision-maker sporadically muddles through
solutions, redefining goals along the way.

The noneconomically rational model stands
against the objective explanation of the environment in which the decision is made. The
decision is made in a subjective environment
constructed by the perceptions and cognitions
of the person. Objective descriptions of the
environment may fail to predict the actual
decision process. If we are to subscribe to
rational choice, then we must rule out selectivity in perception. But selectivity exists
in the perceptual process and may result in
excluding from the decision environment many
variables that would need to be specified when
making a decision using the economic model.
Hence the idea of subjective rationality becomes important when describing decision-making. The decision-maker's bounded subjective
rationality, in an organizational context, is

determined by his limited knowledge of the
world and the organizational environment in
which he lives (March and Simon, 1958).

MODELS OF INDIVIDUAL DECISION-MAKING AND JUDGMENT

The continuum of decision-making can run
from those decisions for which science provides
a normative solution (such as programmable decisions) to those that are totally intuitive.
Interest in both descriptive and normative
approaches to individual decision-making have
led to careful descriptions of the individual
and the environment in which the decision is
made. Decision-making is a complex process,
unique for each individual in accordance with
his perceptual, motivational, and value makeup.
Discovery of the process, however limited in
scope, can have benefits. If a normative model
can be constructed for the decision itself,
the individual's decision can be compared to
the normative model to obtain deviances from
optimality. And, even in the absence of a
normative model, the understanding and description of the decision process can be fed back to
the individual and become a powerful tool for
learning about himself. Further, this feedback
can illuminate and bring to consciousness aspects of decision-making that the individual
was not aware of. We shall describe four different models of human judgment which explain
this process.

MULTIPLE-CUE MODEL

Brunswick (1956) suggested that the perceptual process involves adjustments to the probabilistic cues in the environment. Brunswick's
probabilistic functionalism has been extended
to judgment studies under the name of multiple-
cue or lens model. Given a decision, the
model studies how the available cues are combined by an individual to arrive at a decision,

which is then compared to the optimal decision. Figure 4.2 shows the model in diagrammatic form.

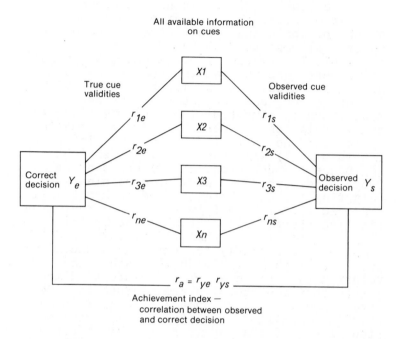

FIGURE 4.2 The multiple-cue lens model.

X_1 to X_n are the *stimulus dimensions*, the cues available in the environment for the decision. If the decision is to select people for a job, then X_1 to X_n would be cues such as age, education, scores on vocational tests, and so on. Based on these cues, the individual makes a decision Y_s. This decision is compared to an optimal solution Y_e obtained through techniques of multiple regression. It is interesting to note how the individual combines cues to arrive at the decision. The observed cue validities are computed by the correlation between the cue values and how in actuality they were utilized. This index can be compared to true cue validities, which are the correlations between the cue values and their real predictive power. If we are interested in selection, we try to see which cues individuals use in deciding whether or not to hire a person. Does he look at the person's age, years of experience, or vocational test scores? Based on previous available information (for example, how personnel experts use the information to make a hiring decision), an optimal hiring solution is determined, and the individual's achievement index is computed. The *achievement index* is the correlation between the judge's actual decision and the optimal decision. The interest is twofold: 1) what aspects of the environment influence the decision, and 2) how can the judge's idiosyncratic ways of combining and weighting the cues be expressed mathematically.

Slovic and Lichtenstein (1971), in reviewing the literature, point out that the most interesting finding is that individuals tend to combine cues linearly to arrive at a decision. Cues are weighted individually rather than in relation to other cues. The failure to demonstrate that configural usage of cues is widespread signifies that humans process information in simplified ways. By *configural* utilization of cues for a judgment we mean that two or more cues are used interactively so that the joint effect is different from the sum of the effects of each cue taken separately. Wiggins and Hoffman (1968) showed that a linear model accurately predicted outcomes for configural judges. However, one should not talk of individual characteristics in judgment irrespective of the task being judged. Even though people tend to be linear judges, the way cues are presented may lead them to make configural judgments (see Mertz and Doherty, 1974).

The multiple-cue model is also helpful as a learning tool. Some judges were asked to describe their own weighting formulae in order to model their insights into their own policy. After the judges made their own decision they were presented with the correct decision. It

was observed that from this feedback process
they learned to utilize cues more appropriately
to arrive at the optimal solution. Linear cues
are the easiest to learn and people are slower
to pick up nonlinear cues. Dudycha and Naylor
(1966) showed that decision makers can learn to
use cues appropriately. However, when a decision maker has one very good cue and then is
given another which is less good, his achievement in decision-making is reduced. Achievement was measured by correlating the actual
decision with the decision that should have
been made. They also found that humans tend to
use cues systematically even when the predictive power of the cues is essentially zero.
For example, suppose an executive is making a
decision about how much to produce. Suppose
that he is given information from past data
on a month-to-month basis on: 1) present inventory, 2) the number of units he should have
produced, and 3) the number of units he actually produced. The best cue is the relationship
between the present inventory and the number
of units he should have produced. The cue
presented by the actual number produced can add
information, but may confuse a strong relationship (for example, the lower the inventory the
more one needs to produce). On the other hand,
giving a cue with medium validity when one of
low validity is available improves performance.
Information is important for decision-making,
but the predictive value of information given
is crucial. Castellan (1974) and Steinmann
(1974) both conclude that various forms of
feedback provided to subjects do not necessarily improve performance or result in transfer.
    Whether information is processed in a simple
linear fashion as predicted by the research on
the lens model, or in more complex ways, has
much to do with the properties of the cues.
If some cues are highly interrelated, individuals combine them and weight them equally
(Slovic, 1966). When presented with a cue
profile, individuals persist in using one cue
if it varies across conditions. Slovic and

Lichtenstein (1971) argue that this occurs because a cue that varies in value allows people to make differential judgments. Although the information is far from conclusive, it seems that the number of cues presented may affect the judgment process. As the number of cues increases, the accuracy of the judgment would be expected to decrease. Slovic and MacPhillamy (1974) have shown that when judgments about pairs of stimuli are made, subjects tend to use cues common to both stimuli rather than those cues that are unique. Common cues provide more comparative information even when the cues do not have high predictive validity. Generally, the research on the multiple-cue model satisfactorily documents man's limitations as an information processor.

THE BAYESIAN PROBABILISTIC MODEL

The job selection problem outlined for the multiple-cue model can be rephrased. Suppose we know that 75% of applicants are usually successful in performing a job. We would now like to use a test for screening applicants. If it is also known that of the successful applicants, 60% score high on the test, while only 30% of the unsuccessful candidates score high, we could determine the likelihood that a person who scores high will also turn out to be a successful candidate. This can be done by using the Bayesian theorem in probability theory. The theorem allows the calculation of conditional probabilities when states of nature are given. Using the previously established (that is, prior) probabilities, the outcome can be judged. The answer to the selection problem would be that about 68% of high scorers would turn out to be successful candidates. The calculation procedure for this can be found in probability texts (for example, see Morris, 1968). If we use the theorem to guide decisions, we are subscribing to an idealized rational approach. Those who work with the Bayesian model suggest that, by using the approach judgments can be analyzed for their optimality. By comparing the actual behavior of individuals in their use of subjective probabilities with the known conditional probabilities of the theorem, the model can be employed to highlight systematic deviations of the actual behavior from the predictions of the model.

Decision-making in this framework aims to identify the hypotheses people have about the environment. The question is, given that one state A exists, what is the chance that B will occur? Given two samples of people S_1 and S_2, with S_1 having predominantly high test scores and S_2 predominantly low test scores, we can compute the probability of drawing from S_1, given that a person is a high test scorer. This is a probability we can derive prior to any information that the decision may yield. If we know the conditions of the environment and we are allowed to see that we had sampled a high scorer, then the probability estimate that it came from S_1 changes. We are now dealing with posterior probabilities, and this is the domain covered by the Bayesian theorem. Posterior probabilities are computed from the prior knowledge about the environment.

The Bayesian theorem gives us the optimal rule about how probabilities would be revised on the basis of new information. If the word "probability" is replaced with "opinion," then we have the possibility of comparing opinion estimates made by individuals with the correct probability that the Bayesian theorem offers. The individual tries to estimate the probability with which an observable datum (for instance, high scorer) is associated to an unobservable data generator (for instance, a sample). Bayesians assume that people can be optimal about the estimates and that they revise their opinions in conjunction with rules specified by the theorem. It is also suggested that when people make such conditional probability estimates, they attain a high degree of internal consistency in their judgments.

Experiments usually ask subjects to give prior probabilities for a set of hypotheses. Then some data is presented (high scorer) and the person is asked to revise his prior opinion about the likelihood of the various hypotheses generating the data. To enable the person to do this revision, he is usually presented with information on the importance of each datum. In the example above, he could be told the number of high and low scorers in each sample. The posterior probability estimated by the subject is then compared to the optimal response obtained through Bayes' theorem.

The general research findings show that, although people estimate probabilities and these are proportional to values obtained using the Bayesian theorem, the proportion is insufficient in amount. This finding is known as conservatism. There is agreement about conservatism, but Bayesians disagree on its explanation. Edwards (1968) summarized three competing explanations: misperception, misaggregation, and artifact. *Misperception* exists when people combine information appropriately but misperceive the diagnostic impact of each datum. *Misaggregation* means that individuals perceive each datum correctly and are aware of its individual diagnostic meaning, but cannot combine its diagnostic meaning well enough with that of other data. In other words, people have difficulty in combining information to arrive at a single response. Peterson (see Edwards, 1968) maintains that conservatism is artifactual and that the complexity of the experiments has produced this phenomenon. Ducharme (1970), in agreement with Peterson, calls this phenomenon *response bias* and contends that Bayes' theorem is a good descriptive model of judgment only for simple tasks. Experiments that describe the judgment process via Bayes' theorem have used very complex tasks. The task requirement for subjects in these experiments is immense. Consider trying to estimate from which urn a sample of 8 red and 4 blue balls comes when the data generators are two urns each having 700 red and 300 blue balls and 700 blue and 300 red balls respectively. Inability to process this information can cause conservatism, thus favoring the artifactual explanation. Some experiments (Phillips and Edwards, 1966) utilize payoffs for improving diagnosticity. It was found that payoffs have a motivating effect and reduce conservatism, although they do not eliminate it. In their review of the literature, Slovic and Lichtenstein (1971) point out that whenever diagnosticity is increased by manipulating the data generator or varying the sample size, the effect is an increase in conservatism. They also found that individuals become resistant to change as available information accumulates. Pruitt (1961) demonstrated that a great deal more information is necessary to change a decision already made than to make a new decision. People may become committed to a hypothesis, and thus be unwilling to change their behavior.

Individuals tend to be consistent in their revisions of probabilities. Summers and Oncken (1968), criticizing the fact that all experiments studying internal consistency of subjective probabilities were limited to the urns and balls type of tasks (what they call neutral tasks), carried out an experiment in person perception. The study was concerned with the logical consistency with which individuals make probabilistic judgments about persons and person attributes. Black and white university students made unconditional estimates regarding: 1) the occurrence of person attributes, and 2) the number of blacks and whites in the population. Calm, moral, unique were types of traits studied. Subjects would be asked to estimate, for example, how many people in a sample of 100 would be moral, calm, unique, black, and white. They were then asked to make conditional estimates regarding all possible attribute-stimulus person pairs. For instance, given a sample of 100 whites, they estimated how many would be calm.

Consistency was measured by the following equation:

$$P(SP)P(A/SP) = P(A)P(SP/A)$$

where the probability (P) of an attribute (A), given a stimulus person (SP), equals the probability of a stimulus person given a trait. The study showed that internal consistency varied as a function of the stimuli; for white stimulus persons, internal consistency was greater than for black stimulus persons. Summers and Oncken concluded that subjects tend toward logical consistency when they make probabilistic judgments regarding persons and person attributes, but consistency is affected by the characteristics of both the stimulus and the respondent. Consistency is influenced by stereotypic and learned beliefs.

EVALUATION OF THE MULTIPLE-CUE AND BAYESIAN MODELS. Both the multiple-cue and the Bayesian approaches are descriptive models of human judgment. Both are concerned with the person who decides and both find that people tend to make suboptimal judgments. In the multiple-cue model suboptimality is shown by the linear effect. This result corresponds to the conservatism findings of the Bayesian model. Both sets of findings indicate the limited information processing capabilities in people.

The multiple-cue model describes how people categorize objects and events. The judgments made are analyzed to determine the cues which are combined to arrive to it. The achievement ratio allows the establishment of a correlation between the person's actual decisions and correct decision obtained from pre-existing information. Whereas the multiple-cue model is purely descriptive, the Bayesian approach is also normative. Bayesians not only explain how a person decides, but also how he *should* decide. In experiments, subjects are asked to choose between outcomes over which they have control. If the subjects use Bayes' theorem

correctly they can always discover the optimal
judgment. Peterson and Beach (1967), reflecting
on Bayesian findings, have suggested that man
operates like an intuitive statistician. When
people make judgments, they approximate a decision that would have been obtained by a
statistical procedure such as Bayes' theorem.
We would tend to disagree with this view on
three counts. First, the research shows conservative findings. Second, the decision tasks
used by Bayesians can confuse the subjects.
Finally, when subjects revise probabilities,
the revision is only sometimes in the right
direction.

The two models have some value as learning
tools. The multiple-cue model can be used to
train people to understand their own decisions.
It can be applied to clinical judgments, to
performance appraisal, to job selection, and
so on. Bayes' theorem deals with scientific
logic and rationality and can be used to increase optimality in judgments by devising
learning tasks based on the utilization of the
theorem. When decisions involving objective
solutions have to be made in organizations, the
Bayesian approach could be useful (see Morris,
1968). For nonprogrammable decisions, the
multiple-cue approach can provide the person
with the understanding of his own unique program to the solution.

ELIMINATION BY ASPECTS

Tversky (1972) suggests that the assumptions
of utility preference based on independence
among choice alternatives are erroneous because
preferences often show dependencies among alternatives. Tversky proposes that each alternative is perceived as being composed of a set of
characteristics, and that choice takes place by
weighing each characteristic. When an aspect
(that is, a characteristic) is selected as
satisfactory, all alternatives that do not
include this aspect are eliminated. A decision
is reached when one alternative survives this

method of elimination by aspects. An example
can be seen in the decision to buy a house.
One can decide as a first aspect that the
price limit for the house is $65,000. All
houses above this price are eliminated, thereby
narrowing the choice. A second aspect chosen
could be that the house must have four bed-
rooms. Again, a number of houses are eliminated. A third aspect could be the requirement
of a family room. This eliminates a few more.
Iteration continues until one is chosen.
Tversky's model represents a way in which the
probability of choosing an alternative can be
understood by the relation of the alternative
to other choice actions. The probabilities in
this model reflect the states of nature at a
given time, and the probability of a choice
alternative increases as a function of the
number of relevant aspects embedded in the
alternative. The model also holds true for
eliminating undesirable aspects. Here choice
involves discarding disadvantageous aspects
and reducing alternatives to the one least disadvantageous. This may be a strategy undertaken
when none of the action outcomes is attractive.

Elimination by aspects is a normative approach to choice, although not a rational one.
It is a decision-making strategy which can be
easily stated and defended by people; it can
also be learned. As we have discussed, people
cannot intuitively compute all probabilities
associated with critical variables in the
decision process. A search quickly results in
a satisficing solution. Elimination by aspects
is attractive as a strategy because one can
justify its use to others. It is normative in
the sense that it suggests how one ought to
decide. However, it is not rational because
there is nothing to ensure that the retained
alternatives are superior to the eliminated
ones. Examples of elimination by aspects can
be seen in commercials in which different
brands of the same product are shown. The an-
nouncer slowly eliminates each brand by an-
nouncing the aspect that the brand does not

possess. We are finally left with the brand that paid for the commercial.

CONJOINT MEASUREMENT ANALYSIS OF HUMAN JUDGMENT

The theory of conjoint measurement (Krantz and Tversky, 1971; Luce and Tukey, 1964) measures the composition rules by which attributes are combined to arrive at a choice. In a decision situation we have alternatives, each of which is composed of several attributes. For example, when we consider the choice of a house we can describe it in terms of price, number of rooms, size of rooms, closeness to schools, closeness to shopping facilities, and so on. In conjoint measurement, we are concerned with discovering the independent effect of each attribute on the ordering of the alternatives. The interest in all judgment theories is in specifying the composition rules by which attributes (other terms used are cues, information, independent variables) are used to predict the value of a choice outcome. However, when it is difficult to measure the attributes by an interval scale, then conjoint measurement is useful because the technique deals with the measurement problem as well as the composition rules by assuming ordinal independence among attributes.

An experiment by Ullrich and Painter (1974) gives us an example of the use of conjoint measurement analysis of human judgment. In this experiment, subjects were provided with profiles of hypothetical applicants for managerial positions. Each profile showed a manager who varied in attributes of intelligence (IQ), years of work experience (E), and achievement motivation (M). The subjects were asked to order their preferences for ten applicants at a time and to rank order each applicant from the most to the least desirable. Analysis of the rankings shows how each subject combined the attributes to arrive at preferences. This analysis provides us with the part-worth contribution, or the utility of each attribute. Ullrich and Painter tested whether an additive composition rule described the judgment made by their subjects. An additive composition rule holds if the overall evaluation of the managers is the algebraic sum of the separate contributions of each attribute level. This can be represented as:

Preference for manager = $f(IQ + E + M)$

They found that one third of the subjects could be classified as using the additive rule. Besides the additive rule, Krantz and Tversky (1971) identify the distributive rule, the dual-distributive rule and the multiplicative rule. In the experiment described above, the use of these rules would generate the following functions:

Preference for manager = $f(IQ+E)M$ distributive rule

Preference for manager = $f(IQE+M)$ dual-distributive rule

Preference for manager = $f(IQEM)$ multiplicative rule

Conjoint measurement is a rather recent development in decision theory. It is a descriptive approach that aims to discover how people use independent attributes associated with a decision choice. Further, conjoint measurement is an axiomatic approach that derives composition rules when people are consistent and follow transitivity of the form $X > Y$, $Y > Z$ implies $X > Z$. The ordering of the choices must be used to order the attributes independently of each other and to satisfy the axiom of ordinal independence. Finally, this model is a qualitative approach because the orderings do not imply numerical values. Conjoint measurement supplements numerical approaches such as the multiple-cue model.

REFERENCES

Brunswick, E. *Perception and the Representative Design of Experiments*. Berkeley, Calif.: Univ. of California Press, 1956.

Castellan, N. J. "The Effect of Different Types of Feedback in Multiple-cue Probability Learning." *Organizational Behavior and Human Performance 11* (1974): 44-64.

Churchman, C. W. *Challenge to Reason.* New York: McGraw-Hill, 1968.

DuCharme, W. M. "A Response Bias Explanation of Conservative Human Inference." *Journal of Experimental Psychology 85* (1970): 66-74.

Dudycha, A. L., and Naylor, J. C. "Characteristics of the Human Inference Process in Complex Choice Behavior Situations." *Organizational Behavior and Human Performance 1* (1966): 110-128.

Edwards, W. "Conservatism in Human Information Processing." In *Formal Representation of Human Judgment,* edited by B. Kleinmutz. New York: Wiley, 1968.

Hirschman, A. O., and Lindblom, C. D. "Economic Development, Research and Development, Policy Making: Some Converging Theories." *Behavioral Science 7* (1962): 211-22.

Krantz, D. H., and Tversky, A. "Conjoint-measurement Analysis of Composition Rules in Psychology." *Psychological Review 78* (1971): 151-69.

Lewin, K.; Dembo, T.; Festinger, L.; and Sears, P. S. "Level of Aspiration." In *Personality and the Behavior Disorders,* vol. 1, edited by J. M. Hunt, pp. 333-78. New York: Ronald, 1944.

Luce, R. D., and Raiffa, H. *Games and Decisions.* New York: Wiley, 1957.

Luce, R. D., and Tukey, J. "Simultaneous Conjoint Measurement: A New Type of Fundamental Measurement." *Journal of Mathematical Philosophy 1* (1964): 1-27.

March, J. G., and Simon, H.A. *Organizations.* New York: Wiley, 1958.

Mertz, W. H., and Doherty, M.E. "The Influence of Task Characteristics on Strategies of Cue Combination." *Organizational Behavior and Human Performance 12* (1974): 196-216.

Miller, G. A. "The Magical Number Seven, Plus or Minus Two: Some Limits on Our Capacity for Processing Information." *Psychological Review 63* (1956): 81-97.

Morris, W. T. *Management Science: A Bayesian Introduction.* Englewood Cliffs, N.J.: Prentice-Hall, 1968.

Myers, J. L., and Fort, J. G. "A sequential Analysis of Gambling Behavior." *Journal of General Psychology 69* (1963): 299-309.

Peterson, C. R., and Beach, L. R. "Man as an Intuitive Statistician." *Psychological Bulletin 68* (1967): 29-46.

Phillips, L. D., and Edwards, W. "Conservatism in a Simple Probability Inference Task." *Journal of Experimental Psychology 72* (1966): 346-57.

Pruitt, D. G, "Informational Requirements in Making Decisions." *American Journal of Psychology 74* (1961): 433-39.

Savage, L. J. "The Theory of Statistical Decision." *Journal of the American Statistical Association 46* (1951): 55-67.

Shubik, M. "Studies and Theories of Decision-making." *Administrative Science Quarterly 3* (1958): 289-306.

Simon, H. A. *Administrative Behavior.* New York: MacMillan, 1947.

_____. "Theories of Decision-making in Economics and Behavioral Science." *American Economic Review 49* (1959): 253-83.

_____. *The New Science of Management Decision.* New York: Harper & Row, 1960.

Slovic, P. "Cue Consistency and Cue Utilization in Judgment." *American Journal of Psychology 79* (1966): 427-34.

Slovic, P., and Lichtenstein, S. "Comparison of Bayesian and Regression Approaches to the Study of Information Processing in Judgment." *Journal of Organizational Behavior and Human Performance 6* (1971): 649-744.

Slovic, P., and MacPhillamy, D. "Dimensional Commensurability and Cue Utilization in Comparative Judgment." *Organizational Behavior and Human Performance* 11 (1974): 172-92.

Soelberg, P. "Unprogrammed Decision-making." *Papers and Proceedings, 26th Annual Meeting, the Academy of Management.* December 27-29, 1966. pp. 3-16.

Steinmann, D. O. "Transfer of Lens Model Training." *Organizational Behavior and Human Performance* 12 (1974): 1-16.

Summers, D. A., and Oncken, G. R. "The Logical Consistency of Person Perception." *Psychonomic Science* 10 (1968): 63-4.

Tversky, A. "Elimination by Aspects: A Theory of Choice." *Psychological Review* 79 (1972): 281-99.

Ullrich, J. R., and Painter, J. R. "A Conjoint-measurement Analysis of Human Judgment." *Organizational Behavior and Human Performance* 12 (1974): 50-61.

Wiggins, N., and Hoffman, P. J. "Three Models of Clinical Judgment." *Journal of Abnormal Psychology* 73 (1968): 70-77.

5

Attitudes

Attitudes are learned predispositions to respond to social objects in a specific manner.
This definition establishes attitudes as
learned hypothetical constructs. A person's
family background as well as his social surroundings and socioeconomic class influence
the attitudes he learns. Many different definitions of attitudes exist in the literature.[1]
Besides the definition given above, attitudes
are also conceptualized as being evaluative,
affective reactions towards objects which:
1) have drive power and give rise to motivational behavior; 2) vary not only in direction
toward an object, but also in strength; 3) are
motivational-perceptual states guided by a
person's selectivity and categorization and
learned through their need-satisfaction properties (Allport, 1955); 4) are relatively stable,
enduring, interrelated entities. Although we
will not attempt to assess the merit of these
different aspects of attitudes, we will

discuss the structure of attitudes and the
functions that attitudes serve for the person.

The discussion will help to establish that
attitudes are complex networks which relate
social objects to one another. Since attitudes
are hypothetical constructs, they are inferred
from observed behavior or they are elicited
through self-reports such as attitude questionnaires. Unfortunately, this gives rise to the
simple concept of attitude as a response to a
stimulus: the social object becomes the stimulus and the response is the score on the
questionnaire. What we obtain is a general
evaluation that the person makes toward an object.

We maintain that the variance in the usage
of the concept of an attitude gives rise to
different techniques of attitude measurement,
each of which ultimately boils down to a stimulus-response measurement. As we list and
evaluate these techniques, we shall note that
a major problem has been the lack of a relationship between the definition of attitude and
the scale constructed to measure it. Preoccupation with the methods to quantify attitudes in
order to give them scientific rigor and ac-
ceptability has focused attention away from the
more important theoretical issues. An important
example is the relationship between attitudes
as hypothetical constructs and actual behavior.
This issue stems from the definition of attitudes as predispositions, an assumption suggesting that people carry predispositions with
them, using the appropriate ones in given situations. In other words, you are predisposed to
react to a situation with behavior that is
congruent with your attitude. For example, if
you have a negative attitude towards your job,
you may show that in your behavior by being
absent. There is wide disagreement about this
assumed relationship between attitudes and behavior. We shall review the evidence for and
against it after discussing the techniques for
measuring attitudes. This will show that a

stimulus-response type of attitude measurement
does not convey the whole process and fails to
tap all underlying dimensions of an attitude.

Finally, we shall look briefly at the theoretical approaches used to study attitudes.
There are various reasons for studying attitudes: for example, to gain a better understanding of how meaning is given to our knowledge; improve communications between people;
and to understand and reduce prejudice. To be
able to do all this often requires that we
change people's attitudes, and thus influence
behavior in desired directions. Attitude change
will concern us in chapter 7.

STRUCTURE OF ATTITUDES

Two approaches to structure attitudes exist
in the literature. One is a three-component
approach known as the affective-cognitive-
conative analysis. The other approach is a
means-end approach which stresses an instrumentality-value analysis. We shall describe
these two approaches.[2]

THE AFFECTIVE-COGNITIVE-CONATIVE ANALYSIS

In this analysis an attitude is described as
having a three-component structure containing
evaluative, cognitive, and conative components.
The *evaluative*, or *affective*, *component* relates to
the favorability with which we regard the attitude issue. It is the main concern of the
attitude and relates to all the emotions evoked
by the attitude issue. The *cognitive component*
refers to the beliefs one has about the attitude object. Anderson and Fishbein (1965) define this component as the belief in the probability that the attitude issue exists, and the
belief about the attitude issue in relation to
other objects, concepts, or goals. Examples of
beliefs would be statements such as "Turks are
fierce," or "toothpaste prevents tooth decay."
Stereotypes are good examples of the cognitive

component of attitude. Beliefs, as well as opinions, and values are all sometimes misused to mean attitudes.[3] The *conative component* refers to the actions taken in relation to the attitude issue, particularly to the statements relating to the attitude issue, that concern the type of behavior that one can or cannot indulge in. For example, suppose the social issue responded to is Indians. Some conative components might be: Indians should be treated as equals; Indians should receive interest-free loans; job opportunities should be provided for Indians. The conative component is sometimes referred to as the behavioral component.

This structural breakdown suggests that two persons having the same attitudes (that is, similar affective components) may vary in their belief about the attitude issue's relation to other issues and in the actions they would take in regard to the attitude issue. People may evaluate pollution as an undesirable state—they have a negative attitude toward pollution. However, they may differ in what they think brings about pollution, and in the means they would use to end it.

The *evaluative dimension* is the summary component of an attitude. It is based on beliefs about the object and its relation to other objects. Often, the evaluative dimension is summarized simply in terms of like/dislike, or favorability/ unfavorability toward the attitude object. This is in accordance with a definition of attitude as an affective tendency to evaluate objects favorably or unfavorably. Although the structure of an attitude is emphasized by most theorists, in actual research they use the evaluative dimension to define and measure an attitude.

INSTRUMENTALITY-VALUE ANALYSIS

In this approach attitudes are described as having instrumental value. Toward certain issues, people have attitudes comprised of the valence of all the goals that the attitude issue is instrumental in bringing about. An *instrumentality-value analysis* of attitude structure suggests that an attitude towards an object is composed of the perceived instrumentality that the object has in relation to the individual's goals and the value that these goals have for him. The person's attitude can be determined by obtaining his perceived instrumentality of the object leading to his goals weighted by his evaluation of these goals (Rosenberg, 1956). To obtain this, the person is first asked to rate the importance of different values. This gives the valence score. Then he is asked to rate whether the attitude object contributes to or blocks the attainment of these values. This gives the instrumentality score.

Attitude is measured as the algebraic sum of the valence of each goal times the attitude object's perceived instrumentality to the goal. For example, one can determine a person's attitude towards refugees. To obtain an instrumentality-value structure analysis, we must do two things. First, measure the importance to the subject of different personal values such as patriotism, education, standard of living, equal rights, and so on. Second, ask the subject how refugees (the attitude object) help or hinder reaching these values. By multiplying the value and instrumentality scores, one should be able to predict the attitude towards refugees that was initially obtained.

Both averaging and additive models of impression formation and instrumentality theories in motivation use a similar conceptual framework. The instrumentality-value analysis is quite valuable, because besides situational constraints that prohibit a certain attitudinal choice, those personal constraints that each individual imposes on himself are taken into account.

FUNCTIONS OF ATTITUDES

The extent to which people have differing

attitudes on a seemingly infinite range of
topics suggests that attitudes serve certain
functions for their psychological well-being.
Katz (1960) and Smith, Bruner and White (1956)
have discussed the idea that attitudes serve
important functions. They argue that attitudes
are maintained because they fulfill social
needs, and they provide an ordering of the
world upon which appropriate responses can be
made. The functional approach suggests that
holding attitudes has a motivational utility.
Knowledge of the functions served by attitudes
is important as it enables us to change attitudes. Different functions may require different change strategies. We shall review four
functions served by attitudes, as summarized by
McGuire (1969).

UTILITARIAN (ADAPTIVE) FUNCTION

This function is in line with a hedonistic
formulation of behavior. We maintain instrumental attitudes that bring about need satisfaction, or we develop unfavorable attitudes
towards objects that frustrate or punish us.
The instrumentality of such attitudes may be
based on past experiences or it may be geared
toward obtaining a certain end in the future.
Smith et al. (1956) talk of a social-adjustment
function of attitudes suggesting that we develop attitudes toward others in terms of the
other's use to us. We also develop attitudes
similar to those held by people we like; the
basis for forming such attitudes is the process
that Kelman (1958) calls "identification." One
develops political attitudes in line with the
party which best serves one's needs. A worker
may develop positive attitudes toward a certain
job because the job is instrumental in satisfying his various needs.

ECONOMY (KNOWLEDGE) FUNCTION

Attitudes are held because they provide order
in a complex world. It is difficult for a

person to make sense of all stimuli impinging on his senses. By categorizing information, the person can come to know his environment more effectively. Incoming information is then weighed against attitude categories and thus evaluated. Smith et al. (1956) call this the object-appraisal function. Stereotypes people hold can be said to serve economy functions.

EXPRESSIVE (SELF-REALIZING) FUNCTION

This is the function served by attitudes when they provide an affirmation of our identity. In this view, attitudes are used by the person to express himself and assert his own identity. In this way a person projects those values he thinks are important to society; he expresses and confirms those aspects of his self-concept that are important. Most of these attitudes develop during the socialization process of childhood when certain values are internalized.

THE EGO-DEFENSIVE FUNCTION

We also develop attitudes to help cope with inner psychological conflicts. We maintain attitudes, not only because they help us evaluate another object, but because they guard us against our own psychological problems. Some of our attitudes are defenses against certain truths or facts we do not like to face. Quite a few attitudes about health issues are of this nature; for example, one develops defensive attitudes towards smoking perhaps because reality is too frightening. Smith et al. (1956) call this the externalization function of attitudes, suggesting that inner conflicts are externalized and used to evaluate objects or people. One may develop hostile attitudes toward businessmen because of unresolved conflicts toward wealth. Derogation of the businessman then protects the person each time the issue of wealth arises. Prejudice toward any object or person usually is frequently a good example of an ego-defensive attitude.

Psychoanalytical theorists have been interested in defensive attitudes and their effects on personality functions (see chapter 8). Ego-defensive attitudes serve adaptive functions as they alleviate the conflict; they are also nonadaptive because they provide a narrower and quite subjective view of the world.

As we have suggested, an understanding of attitudinal functions is important if we are interested in changing attitudes. An attitude serving a knowledge function can be changed by messages with persuasive new communications, whereas attitudes serving utilitarian functions can be changed by influencing the evaluation of the attitude object or the instrumental perception. Expressive attitudes may be changed by providing the person with alternative modes of expression. Ego-defensive attitudes are very resistant to change efforts. In order to change these attitudes, more clinically oriented techniques of influence may be required. This simple paradigm of change often becomes very difficult to operationalize because attitudes may serve multiple functions. A dislike of businessmen may develop as an ego-defensive function but can be bolstered by other, related attitudes so that the person expresses the attitude as one of his important values and thus obtains acceptance by a certain group (such as a certain political party). In this way many functions can be served by the same attitude.

MEASUREMENT OF ATTITUDES

The definition of attitude implies that people differ on a favorable-unfavorable continuum in their reaction toward an attitude issue. People not only differ as to which of the two ends of the continuum they prefer, but also on shades or calibrations of the end of the continuum. Some favor the issue a little and some favor it very much. The notion that people's attitudes can be expressed on dimensions has

led to the development of various means to
measure attitudes. Furthermore the definition
of an attitude implies a predisposition or a
tendency to react. Hence, an attitude may not
always be overtly exhibited, whereas carefully
designed tests may get at these covert attitudes.

When we examine the research literature, we
see that attitudes have been measured in various ways. The variability that exists in
measurement techniques stems from the differing
vantage points of researchers. Psychometricians
have developed very precise and elegant methods
to measure attitudes which have not often been
used by those in attitude research. Many researchers have been quite sloppy in the choice
of statements (called items) they include in an
attitude questionnaire, or in scaling. This
happens because of their hazy definition of
attitude, or because the attitude measure is
not the crucial variable in their study.

Regardless of the confusion that exists in
the area of measurement, we can summarize certain methods which by and large enjoy wide
acceptance as legitimate means of measuring attitudes. One can, based on the manner by which
the attitude measured is obtained, divide attitude measurement into two broad categories:
1) *test measures,* which require the person to
indicate his attitude on a paper-and-pencil
test of some sort; and 2) *behavioral measures,* where
the attitude of the person is indirectly inferred from a supposedly relevant behavior.
Paper-and-pencil tests of attitudes have been
more widely used than behavioral measures because they are simple to construct and easy
to administer. Behavioral measures, on the
other hand, require considerable ingenuity on
the part of the researcher. A problem associated with behavioral measures is the difficulty
of operationalizing the attitude toward the
behavior in question in order to derive a close
correspondence between the measurement and
what the researcher is trying to measure.

A further distinction in measurement is whether the attitude is measured directly or indirectly by disguised means. Testing measures can be of both sorts, whereas behavioral measures are either disguised or are elicited by unobtrusive techniques.

ISSUES IN ATTITUDE MEASUREMENT

There are various issues which may be of concern in measuring an attitude. In designing approaches to measure attitudes one should take into consideration the varying attitude dimensions and devise his measurement instruments in accordance with the kind of information required. The two most important aspects of attitudes are their direction and their strength. The *direction* indicates whether the object is positively or negatively evaluated. The *strength* or *intensity* of the attitude indicates *how* positively or negatively the object is evaluated. Attitudes with a high intensity will be more difficult to change. The strength dimension is therefore important to those interested in attitude change. Most attitude measurement techniques emphasize both the direction and intensity of the attitude measured.

Other interesting features of attitude are its centrality and saliency. Strongly held attitudes are likely to be central to the person's belief and value system. *Saliency* refers to the person's preoccupation with the attitude. In general, centrally held attitudes will be more salient than others. Finally, one may also wish to determine the consistency of one attitude in comparison with others, or how the attitude fits with the person's belief and value system.

TESTING TECHNIQUES FOR ATTITUDE MEASUREMENT

Testing techniques are those approaches that obtain evaluative statements or verbal expressions from people on an attitude issue. Most

of these approaches constitute paper-and-pencil
tests. The interview, which is a technique
wherein evaluative statements can be obtained,
is not accepted as a very efficient or precise technique for data collection. This is
because the interviews can be plagued with
interviewer biases, and they are costly and
difficult to summarize. Paper-and-pencil tests
permit the collection of a large amount of
information in a relatively short period of
time. These tests are also quite economical
to administer. Most scales used in such tests
are based on elaborate and elegant mathematical
rationales. Some paper-and-pencil tests are designed to directly elicit affective statements.
We shall first describe these direct testing
techniques.

DIRECT TESTING TECHNIQUES FOR ATTITUDE MEASURE-
MENT. Direct testing techniques are attempts to
measure attitudes by asking people to indicate
their attitudes on a given issue. The rationale
that underlies this approach is that people
have attitudes they can freely express. If one
accepts this premise, then one can justify
asking people directly how they react toward
a certain issue. Political attitudes, prejudice, and stereotypes have very often been
measured by this approach. Various paper-and-
pencil tests that directly measure attitudes
are constructed by relying on techniques developed by psychometricians interested in attitude scaling. We shall briefly describe the
most widely used scaling techniques as examples of direct testing approaches.

THURSTONE SCALES. The first direct test of
attitudes was a scaling approach developed by
Thurstone (1928). In this approach one begins
by generating statements relevant to the attitude issue measured. Table 5.1 shows some
statements generated to measure attitudes
toward earning a living. It is desirable to
generate over one hundred statements. Each
statement is put on a small card and presented

to a group of judges whose task it is to sort them into eleven piles, ranging from strongly favorable to least favorable toward the issue at hand. After the statements are arranged, those on which there is wide disagreement are discarded. What remains usually are 20 to 30 statements on which there is agreement and which are spread evenly along the continuum. A median score is computed for each, which constitutes the scale value for that statement. The instrument is then ready to be used. The subject is given the final group of statements and is asked to check the statement with which he agrees. The person's attitude is measured by the median scale value of the statements with which he agrees (see Table 5.1).[4]

TABLE 5.1 Some Statements Used by Hinckley and Hinckley's Scale for Measuring Attitudes Towards Earning a Living. This Scale was Constructed in 1939, and Today We Could Surmise that we Would Obtain Different Scale Values for the Statements.

Scale Value	Statement
10.43	The first and most important duty of every man is to earn a living.
8.55	You should earn your living by honest toil.
7.00	I want to work to keep the family out of debt.
4.56	My dream is for a job combining a minimum amount of labor with a maximum amount of wage.
2.19	I never worry about material things such as food and clothing.
0.19	The world owes me a living.

SOURCE: E. D. Hinckley and M. B. Hinckley (1939).

There are certain assumptions made by this technique of measurement. First, it is assumed

that statements can be ordered so that an equal
interval exists on the continuum between ad-
jacent statements. This assumption provides
for the study of the degree of discrepancy
among the attitudes of different people. Second, it is assumed that statements are independent of each other, and thus, that the
acceptance of one statement does not imply
acceptance of others. Third, it is assumed
that the judges sort the items into categories
based on the favorableness toward the issue as
expressed by the statement and not their own
attitudes. That is, **judges** react to the statements in an objective manner without being influenced by their own attitudes on the issue.
All of these assumptions have been seriously
criticized. The third has been empirically
shown to be dubious. Hovland and Sherif (1952)
found that the judges' own attitudes influenced the arrangement of statements. Further
criticisms have focused on the amount of work
required to construct the scale, and on the
fact that two individuals who obtain the same
scale score may be expressing very different attitude patterns. A person who checks an extreme
and neutral item may have the same score as
one checking two neutral items on the continuum. Whether the two have the same attitude
on the issue is clearly debatable.

SUMMATED (LIKERT) SCALES. A very different
approach to direct attitude measurement was
developed by Likert (1932). In this approach,
statements about an attitude issue are generated which subjects can either agree or disagree with. For each statement, the subject
is presented with a scale having five alternatives. A sample item designed according to
this approach would read like this:

I think that older employees make better
employees.
Strongly agree___ Agree___ Undecided___
Disagree___ Strongly Disagree___

The initial list of statements is given to a

group of representative judges who rate their
agreement with each statement. The score for a
statement can vary from 1 (strongly disagree)
to 5 (strongly agree). Each judge's score for
every statement is added to arrive at a final
score. On the average, judges that agree with
the items obtain a high score, and those that
disagree a low score. Let us emphasize that
the numbers associated with the end points on
the scale are arbitrary. Agreement can be assigned either a 1 or a 5. However, these numbers must be consistent throughout the scale.
After the judges' overall scores are obtained,
each statement is analyzed to see whether it
discriminates between high and low scorers on
the attitude issue. Statements that do not correlate with the total score are dropped from
the tests, and a final list of statements, all
of which are related to the same attitude issue, is obtained. This allows for discriminat-
ing between those on the two opposite sides of
the attitude issue.

Since a person's score is obtained by adding
his score on each statement, it is assumed
that each statement is a linear function of the
same attitude issue. Statements are not assumed
to be distinct and independent as is the case
in Thurstone's approach. The scale can be very
different in content from a Thurstone scale on
the same attitude issue. In designing a
Thurstone scale, one is bound by the agreement
of the judges in statement selection, whereas
in a Likert scale one is empirical in statement selection. This provides the possibility
of wider content in a Likert scale. A disadvantage of this method is that it does not
indicate the distance between different attitudes. One learns how people are ranked in
terms of their favorableness toward the attitude issue, but not the degree of favorableness
between persons. Furthermore, the approach is
subject to the same criticism as Thurstone's:
people with the same score can have different
attitude profiles. Finally, both approaches
ignore any structure of opinions. Likert's

approach, however, is simpler and much less time-consuming than Thurstone's.

CUMULATIVE SCALES. The cumulative scales approach is based on the assumption that a single, unidimensional attitude issue can be measured by statements ordered cumulatively along a continuum of "difficulty of accep-tance." In such a scale, when one indicates favorability with statement 2, it is assumed that he is favorable to 1, as well; if favor-ability to 3 is indicated, statements 1 and 2 must also be favored. Those interested in the approach should consult the work of Guttman (1950) who pioneered it.

THE SEMANTIC DIFFERENTIAL. Instead of measur-ing only the favorability of an attitude issue, which largely exemplifies the previous three approaches of attitude measurement discussed, the *semantic differential* provides the person mak-ing the study with numerous dimensions. In this way the technique aims at tapping the structure of the attitude. The approach was developed by Osgood, Suci, and Tannenbaum (1957). The atti-tude issue is presented to subjects along with various bipolar adjective scales (for instance, "hot-cold," "good-bad"). Each bipolar scale typically has seven points. An individual's attitude toward his present employment could be measured on the *semantic differential* in the following way:

My present job

Good __ __ __ __ __ __ __ Bad

Pleasant __ __ __ __ __ __ __ Unpleasant

Active __ __ __ __ __ __ __ Passive

Interesting __ __ __ __ __ __ __ Uninteresting

Scales values range from +3 for positive affect to -3 for negative affect. A person's score is an average obtained from his responses to all scales.

This approach was developed originally to study the "meaning" that people associate with words or concepts. When the bipolar adjective scales were subjected to a statistical technique known as factor analysis, three identifiable dimensions emerged in the semantic space: the *evaluative dimension* (for example, good-bad); the *potency dimension* (for example, strong-weak, large-small); and the *activity dimension* (for example, active-passive, fast-slow). These dimensions provide an approximate understanding of the attitude structure. The *semantic differential* is easy to administer and score. Osgood constructed the instrument for measuring meaning, but many researchers have used it for attitude measurement. Contrary to Osgood's intentions, the *semantic differential* has enjoyed wide usage in fields such as marketing, where it is used to derive consumer evaluations of products.

INDIRECT TESTING TECHNIQUES FOR ATTITUDE MEASUREMENT. Indirect testing techniques refer to those paper-and-pencil tests that try to measure an attitude issue in a roundabout way. This approach is highly desirable if the attitude issue measured is difficult to elicit through direct testing, because people conceal their attitudes, or tend to give socially desirable responses. The assumption of a well constructed indirect paper-and-pencil test is that the respondent is not aware that a particular attitude is being measured. The approach often necessitates that the attitude issue be concealed among a domain of other issues. In such cases, it is sometimes difficult to draw inferences about the particular attitude.

Let us illustrate such a disguised testing approach. Goldberg (1968) measured the attitudes that women had toward women professionals by giving college female subjects articles written by professionals (lawyers, elementary school teachers, dieticians) to rate for style,

clarity, communicative power, and so on. Each
subject received a booklet containing articles
written by six professionals, three women and
three men. Professions included were found in
previous testing to be clearly associated
either with men or with women. The same articles appeared in each booklet, the only difference being that half were described as
written by men (for instance, John McKay) and
the other half by women (for instance, Joan
McKay). Goldberg found that his female subjects
did not evaluate female professionals as positively as they did male professionals. Before
rating the articles a group of women subjects
had ranked occupations to determine those that
were typical for women and men. Even in such
fields as dietetics and elementary teaching,
which turned out to be occupations typically
associated with women, men fared better in
evaluations. The attitude here was inferred
indirectly, from the evaluations of the articles. One would expect that, had Goldberg used
a direct testing approach, he might have obtained quite different attitudinal profiles
because the subjects may have been responding
in a socially desirable way. However, Goldberg's subjects did not know that their prejudices were being measured.

Projective tests used by clinical psychologists, such as the Rorschach or the TAT, are
examples of indirect tests. Achievement motivation, as discussed in chapter 3, was measured
by McClelland using indirect testing techniques. Sentence completion tests have also
been used frequently as examples of disguised
measures.

EVALUATION OF TESTING TECHNIQUES TO ATTITUDE
MEASUREMENT. The criteria by which one should
evaluate any measurement technique are whether
the technique has reliability and validity.
Testing techniques are based on the assumption
that the individual has an attitude towards an
issue which he can articulate. Direct testing
techniques have been widely criticized (Lemon,

(1973). Direct paper-and-pencil tests rely on self reports by the respondents who may give socially desirable responses rather than their true feelings. The investigator may also be a source of bias. By devising a test, the investigator may create an attitude where one did not previously exist, or, by his presence compel the respondent to act in uncharacteristic ways. Further, the investigator's own biases (hypotheses) may lead to tests that are unrealistic in light of the phenomenon studied.

Most of these criticisms are handled by indirect tests. Because they are disguised, they conceal from the respondent the attitude being measured. The problem, incidentally, with indirect tests is that respondents may try to guess what is being measured and give unrepresentative or biased responses; furthermore, there are some ethical issues involved in deceiving respondents. When the validity of indirect techniques is questioned, it appears to be inferior to that of direct attitude scales (Lemon, 1973). However, a danger of the direct attitude measure is that one ends up with a narrow, sometimes circular concept of attitude defined in terms of the measurement instrument. That is, an individual's attitude toward an issue is simply operationalized as his response on a test.

Campbell and Fiske (1959) have argued that to obtain validity in measuring an attitude, various measurement methods should be used, and that the findings of each method should correlate highly with each other when the same trait is measured. Although this suggestion is not often followed, it should be the guide to vigorous research on an attitude issue. A combination of direct and indirect approaches may minimize the error that arises from the use of a single measuring device.

Campbell and Stanley (1963) criticize most paper-and-pencil tests as being *reactive measures* (those that make the respondent aware that he is being tested). Reactive measures may make the respondent anxious since by subjecting him

to a prearranged list of items, they may create
attitudes which formerly did not exist. It is
possible that the mere wording of the tests may
elicit certain response sets. Testing approaches are subject to all these criticisms.
If the respondent's awareness that he is being
tested significantly influences the test results, then behavioral testing techniques that
make use of unobtrusive measures became more
appropriate for attitude measurement. We shall
describe some of the common behavioral measures
of attitudes.

BEHAVIORAL TECHNIQUES FOR ATTITUDE MEASUREMENT

Behavioral techniques use a measure of behavior to infer a person's attitude. This is
usually done in two ways: 1) in an indirect
manner by disguising what is being measured;
and 2) unobstrusively, so that the person is
totally unaware that he is being observed.

PHYSIOLOGICAL MEASURES (DISGUISED BEHAVIORAL
MEASURES). Findings from diverse studies showing that emotional affect states have physiological correlates have been used as justification for behavioral measures of attitudinal
tendencies. This type of measure would not be
subject to social desirability responses and
would give a more direct comprehension of the
internal response. The Galvanic Skin Response
(GSR) is a physiological measure that has occasionally been used in attitude measurement.
The GSR measures the conductance of the skin
to electrical current and is sensitive to
emotional changes taking place within the
organism. This response can be used to measure
emotional reaction to stimuli presented on a
screen, or to people with whom the subject is
interacting.

Another physiological measure of attitude is
that of pupillary size. Early Chinese jade
dealers would try to make a sale based on
their observation of the dilation of the

customer's pupils. Hess (1965) has found that
the pupils dilate with positive affect states
and they constrict with negative affect states.
However, Woodmansee (1970) has not been able
to replicate these results.

Physiological measures seem to be a function
of the arousal level of the respondent. As
such, they may give a better understanding of
the strength of an attitude. The direction of
the attitude may, however, be difficult to
determine from such measures because physiological methods may not distinguish between
different emotional states of positive and
negative affect.

UNOBTRUSIVE MEASURES, Unobtrusive measures
rely on observations of ongoing or completed
behavior. They are not subject to errors
arising from the interaction of the respondent
and the investigator. The problem with the approach is that natural situations in which attitudinal measures might be taken may not occur
with high frequency. Also the approach requires
reliable means of observation of the same
phenomenon by different observers.

Bechtel (1970) devised an apparatus to measure preferences for artwork. With a device
called the hodometer Bechtel was able to determine how much time individuals spent looking
at different exhibits and specific paintings
at a museum. The unobtrusive measure of art
preference accurately predicted the responses
of the museum visitors when they completed
questionnaires tapping their preferences among
the exhibits visited.[5]

A good unobtrusive measure would seem to be
the frequency of behavior. If a person is observed doing something frequently, one can
impute an attitude of affect. If one interacts
with a certain person often, one can deduce
liking, attraction and the like. However,
most unobtrusive measures have serious problems of interpretation stemming from a lack
of control of relevant variables, such as
changes over time in the population studied.

Nevertheless, the nonverbal nature of unobtrusive measures is valuable, as the measures provide information on issues which the respondents often would be unwilling to articulate to an investigator.

ATTITUDES AND BEHAVIOR: IS THERE A RELATIONSHIP?

Perhaps the most important reason for studying attitudes is their assumed relationship to behavior. An attitude is defined as a predisposition to act in a certain manner. This definition implies that if we know a person's predisposition towards a specific issue, we can predict how he will react when he is confronted with the issue. Unfortunately, neither the definition nor the available data can provide such a neat one-to-one relationship where attitudes are causally related to behavior. An attitude, unlike an opinion, is not a response. It is a tendency to respond in a particular way, and even in the definition the probabilistic nature of the relation between tendency and actual response is built in.

An often quoted early study by LaPierre (1934) opened the way to the study of the relationship between attitudes and behavior. In the study, managers and owners of over 200 hotel and restaurant-like establishments had responded on a questionnaire that they would not serve a Chinese couple. However, virtually all (98%) served a Chinese couple who came to their establishment accompanied by LaPierre. This discrepancy between attitudes and behavior has been replicated with other racial groups (Kutner et al., 1952; Minard, 1952). Because there also have been studies positing high correlations between attitudes and behavior (DeFleur and Westie, 1958) many researchers have tried to explain these discrepant findings.

Generally, when researchers seek the relationship between attitudes and behavior, the former is measured by a self-report. The expression of the attitude in itself can be seen as a behavior. In that case, what is being established is the inconsistency between behaviors in two different situations. Even if we restrict ourselves to the notion that the self-report measure of attitude is a measure of behavior, and look at behaviors to which it relates, there are still reasons to expect inconsistency. First, most self-reports measure attitudes toward general stimulus objects, such as blacks or Chinese, whereas in the behavioral situation the respondent usually confronts a specific stimulus object, such as a well dressed Chinese couple speaking fluent English. In such instances it becomes difficult to predict from the general to the specific. This difficulty is accentuated because various external situational factors in the social environment play their part in determining and influencing behavior. Unfavorable attitudes towards blacks will not be exhibited in the behavior of a person who is attending a compulsory course offered by a black professor in order to graduate from college. Actually, many stereotypes and prejudicial attitudes are very rich in belief content but usually have no specific action components related to them. Rokeach (1968) has suggested that a meaningful measure of attitudes should sample the person's feelings toward the attitude object and toward situations involving the attitude object. The male chauvinist boss may have negative attitudes toward working women, but may be in favor of having a very attractive woman serve on the executive board. Second, the constraints under which the person endorses an attitude are often not specified or sampled. Behavior in a situation is limited by personal (that is, internal) and environmental constraints. A person's positive attitudes towards sex may be constrained in a given situation; the partner may have divergent views. Inconsistencies among attitudes and behavior may, to a great extent, be due to the inability or unwillingness of many researchers to identify more clearly the situations in which the attitude object is reacted to, thus allowing the person to choose among alternative forms of behavior while knowing the constraints. This idea is verbalized by Campbell (1963), who suggests that situational hurdles or attitude thresholds make responses at higher levels more and more difficult. Responding to questionnaires asking whether Chinese will be served is an easy hurdle to overcome, but refusing service when the Chinese are physically present has a higher threshold. The face-to-face situation does not elicit the prejudicial attitude that the impersonal questionnaire does.

Finally, difficulties in establishing a correspondence between attitudes and behavior are furthered because a specific behavior may be tied to various, occasionally competing, attitudes. The problem becomes apparent when we sample a general attitude. Very positive attitudes toward cancer research may not result in financial support of a cancer research society if at the same time there are competing favorable attitudes toward providing well for one's family.

Instead of trying to discover whether a relationship between attitudes and behavior exists, it would be easier to study those situations that do or do not exhibit the relation. That would allow a better understanding of attitudes and would help predictions related to attitude change and consequent behavioral change. Even though attitudes are stable, they are open to change. Changing one's beliefs does not, however, lead to a change in one's actions. Many people continue to smoke even though they believe cigarettes are dangerous to their health. However, specifying when and under what circumstances attitudes are related to behavior can suggest those situations where attitude change efforts can be most successful in changing behavior.

STUDY OF ATTITUDES

The process by which attitudes are acquired is quite complex. Most definitions of attitudes explicitly or implicitly characterize them as learned constructs. This suggests that attitudes can be studied within the realm of postulates derived from learning theories. The formation and change of attitudes have been studied using theories guided by principles of conditioning and reinforcement. However, attitudes also have cognitive components. A meaning component is associated with each attitude through which attitudes become interrelated. This has opened investigations that rely on cognitive aspects. Attitudes, as we have already seen, can be studied to determine their functional use. Nevertheless, the functional approach to attitude change has not been useful in providing insights into the change process. Below, we shall briefly note three other approaches to the study of attitudes: 1) conditioning and reinforcement, 2) incentives, and 3) cognitive consistency.

CONDITIONING AND REINFORCEMENT

These approaches use principles of classical and operant conditioning to explain how attitudes are acquired (see chapter 1). Staats (1968) suggests that words can evoke emotional responses if they are paired with unconditional stimuli. Also, the words that work as conditioned stimuli may be associated with new words and by "higher-order conditioning" the new words can evoke emotional responses. Further, learning takes place due to reinforcement. If a verbalized attitude is reinforced, its future expression is more or less secured by the reinforcement. This obvious conclusion from learning theory has received mixed support. Under this framework attitudes can also be acquired through imitation. Significant others elicit attitudes and people,

through imitation, internalize these atti-
tudes.6

INCENTIVES

This view is influenced by hedonic considerations. People hold attitudes that maximize
their pleasure and/or minimize their pain.
There may be positive and negative considerations for any attitude issue. If the positive
considerations outweigh the negative ones, then
the attitude is adopted. You may consider
drugs to be dangerous but exciting; you may
also want to keep your job as an executive.
You will weight these considerations before
developing an attitude toward drugs. Learning
approaches guide much of the incentive formulation. It is, however, difficult to empirically
derive meaningful weights for all elements
considered before an attitude is acquired.
Perhaps this approach best suggests the instrumental nature of attitudes. Attitudes guide
our behavioral choices, based on their instrumentality in obtaining satisfaction and pleasure or minimizing pain and punishment.

COGNITIVE CONSISTENCY

Many varying theories have been labelled
cognitive consistency theories. They all share
the assumption that there is a tendency to
maintain equilibrium among one's cognitions.
This search for consistency influences attitude acquisition as well as the process of
attitude change. These approaches are all motivational in nature, in that they posit a need
for consistency which has drive characteristics. When faced with a situation that provides
information discrepant with their beliefs or
attitudes, people will try to reduce inconsistency between the information and their
attitudes so that an equilibrium is attained.
In a way, these theories accept a homeostatic
formulation. In chapter 7 we shall discuss
these theories in detail.

NOTES

[1]See McGuire (1969) and Scott (1969) for a discussion of different definitions of attitudes.

[2]See McGuire (1969) for a more extended discussion.

[3]See McGuire (1969) for distinctions between the terms.

[4]Techniques for developing and scoring Thurstone scales can be found in Edwards (1957) and Thurstone and Chave (1929).

[5]See Webb, Campbell, Schwartz, and Sechrest (1966) for an enlightening document on various unobtrusive measures used in behavioral sciences.

[6]Hovland and his associates have studied the attitude change process within a broad learning orientation. See Hovland et al. (1953), Hovland (1957), Hovland and Janis (1959), and Hovland and Rosenberg (1960) for examples of the learning approach to attitude change.

REFERENCES

Allport, F. H. *Theories of Perception and the Concept of Structure.* New York: Wiley, 1955.

Anderson, L. R., and Fishbein, M. "Prediction of Attitude from Number, Strength and Evaluative Aspect of Beliefs about the Attitude Object: A Comparison of Summation and Congruity Theories." *Journal of Personality and Social Psychology* 2 (1965): 437-43.

Bechtel, R. B. "Human Movement and Architecture." In *Environmental Psychology: Man and His Physical Setting,* edited by H. M. Proshansky, W. H. Ittelson, and L. G. Rivlin, pp. 642-45. New York: Holt, Rinehart and Winston, 1970.

Campbell, D. T. "Social Attitudes and Other Acquired Behavioral Dispositions." In *Psychology: A Study of Science,* vol. 6, edited by S. Koch, pp. 94-172. New York: McGraw-Hill, 1963.

Campbell, D. T., and Fiske, D. W. "Convergent and Discriminant Validation by the Multitrait-Multimethod Matrix." *Psychological Bulletin 56* (1959): 81-105.

Campbell, D. T., and Stanley, J. C. *Experimental and Quasi-experimental Designs for Research*. Chicago: Rand McNally, 1963.

DeFleur, M. L., and Westie, F. R. "Verbal Attitudes and Overt Acts: An Experiment of the Salience of Attitudes." *American Sociological Review 23* (1958): 667-73.

Edwards, A. L. *Techniques of Attitude Scale Construction*. New York: Appleton-Century-Crofts, 1957.

Goldberg, P. "Are Women Prejudiced Against Women?" *Trans-Action 5* (1968): 28-30.

Guttman, L. "The Problem of Attitude and Opinion Measurement." In *Measurement and Prediction*, edited by S. A. Stouffer, pp. 60-90. Princeton, N.J.: Princeton Univ. Press, 1950.

Hess, E. H. "Attitude and Pupil Size." *Scientific American 212* (1965): 46-54.

Hinckley, E. D., and Hinckley, M. B. "Attitude Scales for Measuring the Influence of the Work Relief Program." *Journal of Social Psychology 8* (1939): 115-24.

Hovland, C. I., ed. *Order of Presentation in Persuasion*. New Haven, Conn.: Yale Univ. Press, 1957.

Hovland, C. I.; Janis, I. L.; and Kelley, H. H. *Communication and Persuasion*. New Haven, Conn.: Yale Univ. Press, 1953.

Hovland, C. I., and Janis, I. L., eds. *Personality and Persuasibility*. New Haven, Conn.: Yale Univ. Press, 1959.

Hovland, C. I., and Rosenberg, M. J., eds. *Attitude Organization and Change*. New Haven, Conn.: Yale Univ. Press, 1960.

Hovland, C. I., and Sherif, M. "Judgmental Phenomena and Scales of Attitude Measurement in Thurstone Scales." *Journal of Abnormal and Social Psychology 47* (1952): 822-32.

Katz, D. "The Functional Approach to the Study of Attitude." *Public Opinion Quarterly 24* (1960): 163-204.

Kelman, H. C. "Compliance, Identification, and Internalization: Three Processes of Opinion Change." *Journal of Conflict Resolution 2* (1958): 51-60.

Kutner, B.; Wilkins, C.; and Yarrow, P. R. "Verbal Attitudes and Overt Behavior Involving Racial Prejudice." *Journal of Abnormal and Social Psychology 47* (1952): 649-52.

LaPierre, R. T. "Attitudes Versus Actions." *Social Forces 13* (1934): 230-37.

Lemon, N. *Attitudes and Their Measurement.* London: B. T. Batsford Ltd., 1973.

Likert, R. "A Technique for the Measurement of Attitudes." *Archives of Psychology 140* (1932).

McGuire, W. J. "The Nature of Attitudes and Attitude Change." In *The Handbook of Social Psychology,* vol. 3, 2d. ed., edited by G. Lindzey and E. Aronson, pp. 136-314. Reading, Mass.: Addison-Wesley, 1969.

Minard, R. D. "Race Relationships in the Pocahontas Coal Field." *Journal of Social Issues 8* (1952): 29-44.

Osgood, C. E.; Suci, G. J.; Tannenbaum, P. H. *The Measurement of Meaning.* Urbana, Ill.: Univ. of Illinois Press, 1957.

Rokeach, M. *Beliefs, Attitudes, and Values.* San Francisco: Jossey-Bass, 1968.

Rosenberg, M. J. "Cognitive Structure and Attitudinal Effect." *Journal of Abnormal and Social Psychology 53* (1956): 367-72.

Scott, W. A. "Attitude Measurement. In *The Handbook of Social Psychology,* vol. 2, 2d ed., edited by G. Lindzey and E. Aronson, pp. 204-73. Reading, Mass.: Addison-Wesley, 1969.

Smith, M. B.; Bruner, J. S.; and White, R. W. *Opinions and Personality.* New York: Wiley, 1956.

Staats, A. W. *Learning, Language and Cognition.* New York: Holt, Rinehart and Winston, 1968.

Thurstone, L. L. "Attitudes Can Be Measured." *American Journal of Sociology 33* (1928): 529-54.

Thurstone, L. L., and Chave, E. J. *The Measurement of Attitude*. Chicago: Univ. of Chicago Press, 1929.

Webb, E. J.; Campbell, D. T.; Schwartz, R. D.; and Sechrest, L. *Unobtrusive Measures: Nonreactive Research in the Social Sciences*. Chicago: Rand McNally, 1966.

Woodmansee, J. J. "The Pupil Response as a Measure of Social Attitudes." In *Attitude Measurement*, edited by G. Summers, pp. 514-33. Chicago: Rand McNally, 1970.

Attribution

Attribution theory looks at how we ascribe cause to the human behavior we observe, a process closely related to perception. When we observe someone interacting in a social situation we not only attempt to form an impression of his traits, but also to dissect his behavior in order to get a feeling of what forces cause the person to behave in the way he does. The inference of causality is a search for what Heider (1958) calls stable dispositional properties. *Stable dispositional properties* are tendencies to behave the same way in a wide variety of situations. For example, if we see someone assuming authoritative postures and giving orders, we may conclude that he has a dispositional property of dominance that causes him to behave this way. The inference of dominance forms the basis of the attributional process, wherein we attribute causes to someone's acts. This inference process is

conditioned by the situation in which it takes
place and by the actors and observers involved.

We shall be concerned with two general kinds
of attributions: 1) *personal causation*, or those
instances when people attribute the cause for
a behavior to internal dispositions, that is,
to personal reasons and dispositions; 2) *environmental causality*, or those instances where
the cause for a behavior is attributed to the
external environment.

Personal causation will be discussed from two
vantage points. First, we shall look at how we
infer personal causality for the behaviors we
observe in others. A model that traces attribution from an action back to dispositions will
be summarized and applied to attributions of
ability, attitudes, responsibility, and trust.
Second, we shall see how we attribute cause to
our behavior. In discussing self-attribution
we shall note that, as actors, we tend to perceive different causes than do observers of
the same situation.

Under environmental causality we shall explain a theory that shows how we infer the
stable features of the environment in order to
attribute a cause to a situation while ruling
out personal causation.

We shall argue that attribution, as detailed
by these models, is a complex process of inference. It may be that the models are too elegant and complex to be realistic. In organizations people make attributions only when the
behavior of co-workers has personal relevance
for them. The conditions under which people
become involved in attributions in organizations are listed briefly at the end of this
chapter.

PERSON PERCEPTION AND ATTRIBUTION THEORY

Heider's (1958) seminal work on attributional
processes has influenced many to enlarge and
broaden his ideas. His approach is based on
what he calls naïve psychology. In his view,

people understand each other by describing how
they perceive their social world. These descriptions use everyday language to portray
the hypotheses the person has developed about
others. We have explained this in our discussion of implicit personality theory. Heider
further assumes that the usage of this naïve
psychology enables people to predict their
environment. Since the environment to be predicted contains objects and persons, Heider
holds that similar processes govern the prediction process for objects and behaviors of
others.

A difficulty we encounter in the process of
perception is the determination of the properties of an object of perception when the environment in which it exists has wide variability. Brunswick (1956) referred to the perception process as probabilistic functionalism.
Perceptual constancies that allow us to see
invariant objects under variable environmental
conditions operate probabilistically. Heider
argues that a similar process holds for person
perception. A behavior should not necessarily
be attributed to an enduring dispositional
property of the actor because it can be a
manifestation of different dispositions. Thus,
when someone gives orders, he may do so out of
a dispositional property of dominance, as well
as one of hostility. In extending Brunswick's
approach, Heider proposes that an observed behavior is only probabilistically related to a
dispositional property of the actor.

Heider's central thesis is that an observer
perceives behavior as being caused. When describing the conditions in which causality
is perceived, his concern lies in establishing
phenomenologically whether the locus of
causality is internal to the person or rests
in the environment. DeCharms (1968), looking at
causation from a motivational viewpoint, suggests that man strives to be a causal agent.
In coming into contact with his environment,
man becomes motivated to produce changes, to be
efficacious. In other words, DeCharms

posits an inherent motive for personal causation.

This notion of internal and external causality is not new to us. It was introduced when discussing motivation. If a person feels he is the *origin* of his behavior we assume that he will attribute causality to himself, whereas a person who sees himself as a *pawn* of the situation will tend to attribute causality to his environment. Rotter (1966) and DeCharms (1968) suggest that if people perceive an internal locus of causality for their behavior, they assume responsibility for their acts. The models of personal and environmental causality that we shall describe are closely tied to the process of perception.

PERSONAL CAUSATION

When a person acts, his behaviors produce effects. The effects may be due to his personal efforts and to environmental forces present during the act. When he behaves in a certain manner the effect due to his personal efforts comes from what he can do and how hard he tries to do it. In other words, the personal component of the effect of a behavior is composed of the person's abilities and of his trying. To be able to attribute personal causality, we must know something about the person's intention. Does he want to behave in a particular manner? Is he capable of behaving as he wishes? In trying to understand the conditions under which we can infer personal causality, we must establish that there are no environmental constraints on a person's behavior. If a person has volition, that is, if he is free to choose among alternative courses of action, then we can infer personal causality and rule out external reasons for his behavior, assuming he has the ability to act and he tries to bring about the effect. Inference of personal causality leads us in turn to attribute stable dispositional properties to the person. In the

next two sections we shall explain how we infer
dispositions in others and in ourselves.

FROM ACTS TO DISPOSITIONS

Jones and Davis (1965) have developed a model
to explain the way in which we infer dispositions from observed acts. They start by assuming that perceivers seek to find *sufficient* reason for the causes of behavior. Instead of approaching the exercise of causal attribution
scientifically, the perceiver is satisfied
when he can assign an intention or a motive
to the behavior. His search for an explanation
ends when a satisfactory intention is found.

In inferring the cause of an act, knowledge
and information about the effects of the act
are very important. If we know that the effects
of a person's behavior were accidental we cannot infer personal causality. Besides having
knowledge of consequences, we also must know
whether the person is able to produce certain
effects and if he wants (tries) to produce
these effects. Ability, of course, often can be
constrained by the environment. If a task is
too easy or too difficult, it is sometimes
difficult to infer personal causality. For example, suppose you are watching a man playing
pool. Some shots are very easy and some, such
as a three cushion call shot, are extremely
difficult. It is hard to infer his skill if you
only observe easy shots being made. But if he
makes a very hard shot, you may conclude that
he was very lucky rather than skillful. To assess his skill you would need many observations
of his playing. According to Jones and Davis,
knowledge and ability are the preconditions
necessary for the assignment of intentions.
If we assign intentions, then we can infer
the underlying stable dispositions. This important process was emphasized by Heider when he
stated that people try to minimize the in-
variance in others' actions, so that they can
predict their environment better. Schematically,
the Jones and Davis model is shown in Figure 6.1.

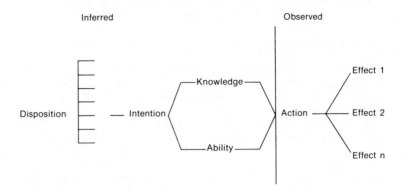

SOURCE: E. E. Jones and K. E. Davis (1965).

FIGURE 6.1 The action-attribute paradigm.

Let us trace Figure 6.1 with an example. While working in a department of an organization you observe the head of the department hire a new employee. This action is accompanied by a few effects, such as less work for everyone involved, and the fear of being fired because a new person has been added to the department. By his action, the department head has the ability to cause both effects. If you decide that he also has knowledge of the effects caused by his acts, then you can decide that he may have intended these effects. Having once established his intention, the employees may then infer his disposition. They may infer that the department head is thoughtful and considerate if they noticed only the first effect; that is, everyone can work less; but if they fear that the new employee will ultimately replace them, they may infer authoritarianism and connivance.

The major variable of the theory is *correspondence*, the relation that exists between the act and the intention when they are described by a similar inference. Correspondence exists when the perceiver assigns the right intention

to the actor's behavior and the dispositional
property explains it as well. We should bear
in mind that intention and dispositions are
person-attributes. They account for action
only when the environment is free from constraints. When settings impose constraints on
actions, the correspondence of inference de-
clines. Hence, correspondence is a concept
dealing with attribution of personal causation.

A crucial tenet of the theory is the way in
which correspondence is determined. Correspondence has two determinants. First, it is important to determine whether the act has *socially
desirable* effects. If we observe someone whose
behavior has socially desirable effects, it
does not tell us much about him. Suppose a
person gives his seat on the bus to a pregnant
woman. This action has socially desirable effects but is also culturally stereotyped. The
observer would infer that most people, including himself, would behave in a similar
fashion under the same circumstances. Only
when the effects of a socially desirable behavior are negative (for instance, when help
becomes hindrance) can we determine correspondence. Various perceptual biases, such as
stereotypes, enter the inference process and
make socially desirable behaviors less predictive of intentions and disposition. Second,
one has to look at the alternative avenues of
actions available to the actor. Each action
usually has a number of potential effects. To
understand the cause behind an action, we must
look at the common effects shared by all alternative actions and the number of *noncommon
effects* caused by the chosen action. The more
noncommon effects caused by the chosen action,
the less the information we have about the
person.

Let us illustrate the calculation of noncommon effects with an example. Suppose a person
has a choice between two executive jobs in two
organizations O_1 and O_2. Both organizations
are large and offer a good salary. Either job
will provide the person with prestige and

status. O_1, which boasts of an open, democratic atmosphere among all employees, is
situated in a small town which is warm
throughout the year. O_2 has a paternalistic,
authoritarian view toward employees and is
situated in a large city which also has a
warm climate. The noncommon effects (see
Figure 6.2) for O_1 are that it is a democratic
organization in a small town. The noncommon
effects for O_2 are that it is an authoritarian organization located in a large city.
These noncommon effects help us draw an inference about the person. If O_1 is chosen we
may infer that the person is open, liberal,
quiet, and relaxed. If the person chose O_2
we could infer that he is traditional, dogmatic, active, and seeks stimulation.

The highest correspondence of inference
occurs when the effects of the act are low
in deisrability and when the act causes few
noncommon effects. In a study (Jones et al.,
1961) testing this proposition, a situation
was set up in which subjects heard a tape
recording of someone being interviewed for
a job. The subjects were told the role requirements of the job. On the tapes they
heard interviewees either behaving along
the role requirements of the job or not.
When subjects were asked to evaluate the
interviewees, they had an easy time with
those not behaving along the role requirements. Such out-of-role behavior has both
socially undesirable effects and few noncommon effects which facilitated making attributions. However, subjects expressed difficulty in inferring dispositions for those
behaving as demanded by the job. When asked
how confident they were in the attributions
they made, subjects displayed high confidence
for out-of-role behavior, but little confidence for in-role behavior.

Two other variables can influence correspondence if the actor's actions contain effects
relevant to the perceiver. First, if the effects of the action produce gains or losses for

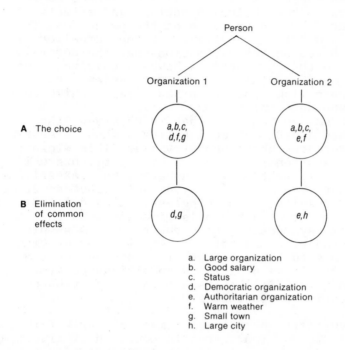

a. Large organization
b. Good salary
c. Status
d. Democratic organization
e. Authoritarian organization
f. Warm weather
g. Small town
h. Large city

SOURCE: E. E. Jones and K. E. Davis (1965). p. 256.

FIGURE 6.2 Determination of noncommon effects for inferring choice of a job.

the perceiver then they have a motivational significance which the authors refer to as *hedonic relevance.* Hedonic relevance increases correspondence because it tends to diminish the noncommon effects. Halo effects can also occur because of hedonic relevance. When an actor's behavior has direct effects on the perceiver, then through a process of cognitive evaluation the perceiver will tend to group actions and their effects into "good and bad for me." Hedonic relevance increases the correspondence of inference. Second, there is the variable of personalism tied to hedonic relevance which also increases correspondence. *Personalism* refers to the choice of actions and effects affected by the presence of the perceiver. This is a difficult judgment for the perceiver. It is based on the assumption that the actor is aware that his actions have a positive or negative effect on the perceiver. Relevance and personalism, when combined, lead to high correspondent inferences.

From one behavior that is observed, the Jones and Davis model builds a whole tree of inferences about unobservables. This elegant explanation is supported by experiments which we shall next review. However, most experiments control so many of the variables that sometimes the results are meaningless. It is difficult to believe that a person's mind works in the complex ways described by the theory. A simpler explanation may offer itself in many attribution situations. If we like someone's actions we attribute positive dispositions to him and if we dislike his actions we attribute negative dispositions.

ATTRIBUTION OF ABILITY. Imagine yourself in a task force. Your group is composed of five members and must come up with a report within a given time. Your reward is very much dependent on the group's performance. As the group proceeds in the task, you notice that one member's behaviors are not conducive to task performance; that is, while the group works on the task, this one member's behavior leads the group to make mistakes, to fail in meeting timetables, and so on. How would you judge that person? We know that quite interesting group norms and pressures may develop against that individual, but our interest is only in attributing dispositions to the person. There are two variables to take into consideration in trying to infer the person's disposition from his actions; first his ability, and second his motivation towards the task. If you know that the person has the ability for the task, then you may infer that he is not

motivated to work. For example, you may have
worked with him on a similar task in the past
and know that he has the ability. At this
point, an inference of laziness as a dispositional property may be made because the member
is not trying hard enough. If his work also
hinders the attainment of rewards for the group
he may be less liked.

Similar results were obtained in an experiment by Jones and DeCharms (1957) in which a
confederate who was a member of a group constantly failed at the task. In one condition
of the experiment, the failure of the confederate did not interfere with the other members'
attainment of their rewards. Opposed to this
individual fate condition was a common fate
condition, in which the confederate's failure
prevented all members from obtaining rewards.
An additional variation was included that cut
across these conditions. Half of the subjects
were led to believe that the confederate's
failure on the task was due to his inability.
The other half of the subjects were told that
the confederate's lack of success on the task
was due to the group's lack of success on the
task and that the group should try harder.
Here is another example of the hedonic relevance variable at work. The confederate's
actions have gain or loss implications for the
perceivers. Table 6.1 shows the results of the
experiment. In the common fate condition, when
the confederate lacked motivation, he was
rated low on traits of competence, dependabili-
ty, intelligence, likeability. However, if he
was seen as not having the ability, he was not
evaluated negatively in the common fate condition. The ratings for the individual fate condition were the same as those of common fate,
when the confederate lacked ability. Lack of
motivation in the individual fate condition
resulted in much less negative evaluation than
in the common fate condition. In the latter
condition, hedonic relevance was important.

Supervisory behavior can give us many clues
as to the attributions of ability and effort

TABLE 6.1 Jones and DeCharms (1957) Study on Ability Attribution.

	Common Fate	Individual Fate
Lack of Ability	17.3	18.9
Lack of Motivation	23	14.4

The scores reflect an index of different traits such as competence, intelligence, likeability. The higher the score the more negative the evaluation.
SOURCE: E. E. Jones and R. DeCharms (1957).

while at work. This is an area which applies directly to the attribution process. Will a supervisor pay more attention to his workers when he knows they have the ability to perform but lack the motivation to do the work? How will supervisors combine reward-punishment contingencies based on the inferences they make about their workers' dispositional properties? Some studies give us clues to these questions from an attributional viewpoint. Rothbart

(1968) found that highly motivated supervisors
used more rewards and fewer punishments than
less motivated supervisors. When the highly
motivated supervisors used rewards and their
workers failed, they were less willing to infer a lack of motivation in their workers than
were those supervisors who used punishment.
Highly motivated supervisors assumed that
their workers lacked ability. In another study
(Lanzetta and Hannah, 1969), it was found that
supervisors were more inclined to punish the
failure of those subjects who had high ability
than those with low ability. When a person
fails, not because of inability but because he
does not try, we may hold him more responsible
for his failure and punish him because we are
frustrated.

Jones et al. (1968) found an interesting
primacy effect in the attribution of ability.
They had a subject and an accomplice take a
rigged IQ test. The items were quite difficult
and some were insoluble. False feedback was
provided to the subject about his and the
accomplice's performance. In one condition,
subjects were told that the accomplice had
solved 15 randomly scattered problems out of
the 30. In another condition, the accomplice
had solved 15 problems, but most of them were
the initial ones. In a third condition, the
accomplice again solved 15 problems, but had
more success toward the end. When the accomplice was more successful at the beginning
than at the end, he was perceived as more
intelligent. Subjects also distorted his test
performance in a more favorable direction and
predicted he would do better in a future
series. This suggests that observers attribute
ability early in interactions. Late successes
may be interpreted more as motivational efforts.

ATTRIBUTION OF ATTITUDE. When interacting with
another person, we always try to figure out
their beliefs and attitudes. Knowing what people
really believe seems to benefit decisions for

future interactions. A member of an ethnic
group undergoing a job interview finds it
helpful to know whether or not the interviewer
is prejudiced. It is important for him to figure out whether the all-smiles face and liberal
stance taken by the interviewer toward his
ethnic membership really reflect his true
feelings or if they are a facade, attributable
to the pressures emanating from the interview
situation. External attributions of attitudes
are usually made when strong environmental
forces are seen to reflect in the actor. In
the absence of such forces, feeling and attitude statements are accepted as genuine. You
would expect this result when using the correspondent inference model.

Jones and Harris (1967) tested the notion
of attitude attribution by having subjects
estimate a stimulus person's attitude toward
Castro from a speech written by the person.
The speech either favored or opposed Castro,
and the stimulus person either was assigned
to write it for the debate team or had chosen
to write it. In terms of the theory of correspondent inferences, the person who writes
either a pro or an anti statement without
choice does not give many clues about his
behavior. Choice, however, narrows down the noncommon effects. Subjects thought that the
person had pro-Castro or anti-Castro attitudes
when he himself had chosen the side he wanted
to defend in the debate. Such confident and
strong attributions were not made for those
who had no choice.

ATTRIBUTION OF RESPONSIBILITY. In the beginning of this chapter we established that people
are motivated to produce effective changes in
their environment. This suggests that people
are often held responsible for their actions.
A person is held responsible for any effects
emanating from an action he intended and also
from actions he is able to create. A person
is not held responsible for acts resulting
from forces external to him. An intention,

which is necessary for attributing responsibility, is an internal event which cannot be
directly observed. Actions are therefore necessary for attributing intent.

Walster (1966) looked at the effects of an
outcome on the assignment of responsibility.
Her subjects listened to a tape recording describing an incident where a young man's car
accidentally rolled down a hill. Walster used
two conditions in the study: there was either
much or little damage to the car, and the car
either came close to hitting a man and a
child or actually hit them. The worse the
consequences of the accident, the greater was
the responsibility assigned to the young man.
This study indicates that, as it relates to
the attribution of responsibility, hedonic
relevance and personalism increase correspondence. The study also points out that the
magnitude of the effect of an act influences
responsibility attribution. If the misfortune
arising from an act is minor, the responsibility attribution to the originator of the act is
overlooked. A serious consequence, on the other
hand, requires at least a responsible scape-
goat. It is not unusual to find responsibility
attributions made constantly in organizations
when something consequential goes wrong. Fault
is found because someone should have double-
checked, looked things over, and so on.

ATTRIBUTION OF TRUST. An important issue in
organizational behavior is that of trust.
Supervisors confront the issues of trustworthiness whenever they must be away from the job.
Should they trust the workers they leave un-
attended? Obviously, each work situation brings
about its own determinants of interpersonal
trust. Nevertheless, trustworthiness is a
dispositional property which supervisors decide
their workers either do or do not possess.
Let us look at the components influencing an
inference of trust. Strickland (1958) tried to
find out whether or not trust is related to
amount of surveillance. In an experiment, a

subject supervisor was able to supervise closely the work of one worker but not that of a
second worker. The supervisor's job was to obtain high performance from his workers on a
monotonous task. Although each worker performed with equal success, when given the
choice of whom to monitor in subsequent trials,
supervisors always chose the worker whom they
had previously monitored for future supervision. Supervisors in this study made different attributions to the monitored and nonmoni-
tored workers. The worker who was not super-
vised was seen as working hard because he
wanted to, whereas the monitored worker was
perceived as less trustworthy. It is interesting to note that a responsibility attribution
is also being made in this instance. The
supervisor takes responsibility for the work
of the monitored worker and thus justifies
the distrust attribution. In similar experiments, Krunglanski (1970) replicated Strickland's findings.

PERCEIVING THE CAUSES OF ONE'S OWN BEHAVIOR

The process of attribution we have discussed
illustrates some of the rules governing a perceiver's attribution of personal causality to
the behavior of those around him. The other
side of the coin is also intriguing; that is,
how do actors themselves attribute cause to
their behaviors? We turn to theories that explain how individuals assign causality for
their own acts.

SELF-ATTRIBUTION. Bem (1967) has proposed what
some call a radical model of self-attribution.
He suggests that we often engage in behaviors
and afterwards ask ourselves, "Why did I do
that?" The answer is obtained much like attributing cause to another actor's behavior,
just as Jones and Davis (1965) proposed. The
difference is that the actor and the observer
are the same person, ourselves. Bem's analysis
delves into the relationship between attitudes

and behavior. We behave in a certain manner towards an entity and then deduce the attitude we hold towards the entity. Bem introduces the notion of tacted and manded behaviors. *Manded behaviors* are in response to the situation. They are commanded, requested, or demanded from the person. This is a social judgment wherein an existing reward or punishment contingency leads the person to judge whether or not the action was manded by the situation. The notion is similar to Jones and Davis' argument of social desirability. If it is judged that most people would have reacted to the situation, one cannot easily infer a personal disposition. A *tacted behavior*, on the other hand, is not in response to a specific situation. It is behavior shaped and reinforced by a past history enacted under neutral situational determinants. Tacted behaviors allow for dispositional inferences.

DIFFERING ATTRIBUTIONS OF THE CAUSES OF BEHAVIOR BY ACTORS AND OBSERVERS. All too often in an organization, when a worker tells his superior that his work has been poor because he has had to cope with a stressful situation at home, the supervisor believes instead that the failure has been due to the worker's disposition—to his laziness or inability. Jones and Nisbett (1971) have suggested that the same behavior leads to divergent perceptions of its causal nature by actors and by observers. They propose that actors use more situational attributions and observers use more dispositional attributions. There is a tendency for a person to explain his behavior by the situational, environmental, external requirements of the context of behavior, whereas an observer watching the same person act attributes the causality to personal factors, inferring stable dispositional properties of the actor. The authors argue that this state of affairs exists because the information available to the actor and the observer are not always identical and because the actor

and observer process information differentially.

There are three kinds of data that actors
and observers can consider in the attribution
process. First, there is *effect data* which
deals with the effects that the action has
created. Basically, there are three broad
types of effect data: 1) information about the
nature of the act itself; 2) information
about the environmental outcomes of the act
(such as, success or failure); and 3) information about the actor's experiences (anger,
satisfaction). Although both observer and
actor can be cognizant of what was done and
what were the environmental outcomes of the
act, the observer cannot directly know the
experiential states of the actor. The observer
can only infer these internal states from nonverbal clues or by knowledge of how he and
others feel in a similar situation. Second,
there is *cause data*, which can be divided into
two broad types: 1) environmental causes (like
rewards), and 2) information on intentions.
The observer can have the information on environmental stimuli operating in a given context just as the actor does. However, intentions are inner states. They are not observed
directly and the observer's knowledge of them
is subject to error. A third category of data
is *historical data*. The actor will not make a
dispositional attribution to his behavior because he knows his past history and may feel
the cause lies in the situation. An observer
usually does not have access to historical
information about the actor. For example, he
sees a person who is helpful and takes that as
a typical sample of behavior.

Jones and Nisbett (1971) suggest that observers and actors use different scales of
comparison when evaluating an act. A person
judges his actions in reference to his past
rather than to acts of other people. Analysis
of their acts suggests that actors and observers may share the same informational base
regarding the external, directly observable

referents of actions, but actors have more and more precise information about the internal referents of actions.

Actors and observers process the information available to them from different perspectives and this affects the outcome of their attribution processes. The actor, while acting, cannot observe and monitor his own behavior very closely. For the actor, the environmental context is most salient. This usually results in the actor attributing his behavior to situational properties. The observer, on the other hand, looks at behavior. For him, behavior stands as the figure on the environmental ground. This effect is heightened by the case where the observer is not merely passive but interacts with the actor. His presence, as part of the environmental context, affects the actor. However, the observer and the actor share the environment of the act, and the observer imputes dispositions to the actor when the actors behave differently in the same situation.

Let us briefly note that this analysis departs slightly from that of Bem (1967). He emphasized that people use the same kind of inference process whether they are attributing cause to themselves or to others. Jones and Nisbett agree with this position, but stress that actors self-attribute more environmental causes for their behaviors, and observers more dispositional causes.

When discussing the attribution of ability we explained a study by Jones et al. (1968) in which a subject and accomplice took an IQ test, and the subject was given false feedback on the accomplice's score. The subject always tended to attribute a dispositional property to the accomplice, such as ability. The study also investigated the different attributions that actors and observers make for the same behavior. In two other conditions of the experiment, subjects received feedback on their own performance. As with the accomplice feedback conditions, subjects received feedback

suggesting that they had done well in the initial problems or that they had done well in the
final problems and that all items were of similar difficulty. Subjects who were successful
in the beginning felt that problems became
more difficult, and subjects who were successful at the end thought that problems became
easier. These perceptions affected their predictions of how well they would perform in a
future series. Ascending performers predicted
they would do better in the future than did
descending performers. This is a reversal of
the prediction that they had made when they
were observing others who had previously under-
gone what they now experienced. When observing
the unknown accomplice in the same situation,
they had predicted that descending accomplices
would perform better in the future because the
observers were inferring the disposition of
ability. When inferring the cause of their own
behavior their judgment of their ability was
unaffected. They attributed their performance
to the difficulty in the task.

The best test of the Jones and Nisbett
hypothesis about actors and observers was made
by Storms (1973). Storms hypothesized that
actors attribute cause to situational factors
while observers attribute cause to dispositional factors. This happens because different information is available to each party and because each processes information differently.
He reasoned that if actors could have the
information available to the observer they
might reverse the nature of their attributions.
The same should hold true when observers are
given information unavailable to them. Storms
analyzed situations where two subjects desig-
nated as actors were asked to spend five
minutes getting acquainted. Each actor was assigned to an observer subject who watched his
assigned actor during the interaction. Data
collected through trait ratings demonstrated
that actors attributed the causes of their own
behavior to situational characteristics, whereas observers reported dispositional

attributions. However, in one condition of the experiment the actors were able to view themselves and observers saw the other participant with whom their actor was conversing. The previous results were reversed in this condition. Actors watching themselves attributed cause to their own dispositions and observers watching the other participant attributed cause to situational characteristics.

ATTRIBUTION AND EVALUATION OF OTHERS

The process of inferring causality is crucial in human interaction because an important outcome of an attribution bears on how we evaluate another person. Even in a short lived interaction we form impressions of another person and, as observers, we infer that the other has dispositional properties. Concurrently, the kinds of dispositions we assign to others will influence our evaluations about them. Smiles, taken as a disposition of friendliness, lead us to like a person. Helping, when seen as an altruistic disposition, leads to admiration. A person who threatens may signal his authoritarian disposition and this may cause an observer to have negative feelings about him. When two people who have the same power interact, dispositions can be inferred on each side and positive and negative evaluations can be made accordingly. On the other hand, if those interacting in the situation have unequal status, the dispositions inferred are marred by that perception, and evaluations are affected consequently.

INGRATIATION AND LIKING. Jones (1964) defines *ingratiation* as tactics used by a person to make himself attractive to another. The person who has less power in an interaction may resort to such tactics. For example, let us suppose someone is complimented for a job, both by a subordinate and by a colleague from another department who has no jurisdiction over him The compliments are both examples of

positive personalism and they are beneficial
to the recipient. The person, however, would
probably like to know whether his worker really thinks highly of him, or if he is being
ingratiating in order to make himself attractive and obtain favors in the future. Inferring good intentions from his colleague's
compliments is simpler. The colleague has equal
status, no interest in the person's affairs,
and it is easier to believe that he speaks his
mind.

Thibaut and Riecken (1955) had subjects work
with two accomplices, one of whom had higher
academic and social status than the subject.
The other accomplice had lower status. During
the experiment the subject realized that he
needed the help of both confederates and, following the experimenter's encouragement, requested help. Both confederates complied with
the subject's request. At this point the subject was asked to explain why the confederates
complied and was asked to evaluate them. The
high-status confederate's intentions were seen
as beneficial because he could easily refuse
the request to help. The low-status confederate did not have that much choice and felt
more obliged to help. The high-status person
was perceived as more attractive. The study
also suggested that power influences the perception of causality. The person who has high
status is seen as complying because of personal
causation. He wants to help. The low-status
person's compliance is seen as externally
caused. He replies to the pressure put on him
by complying with the request.

Environmental Causality

In our discussion of personal causation we
saw examples in which people attributed the
cause of their actions to situational determinants of the context in which the observed
behavior was transacted. A person perceives
behavior as being internally caused only when

the situational forces are not too compelling
and when he has the ability to deal with them.

We now turn to a model that explains the
conditions under which clearcut external attributions are made. Kelley's (1967, 1971)
work complements the Jones and Davis (1965)
acts-to-dispositions model discussed previously.

EXTERNAL ATTRIBUTIONS: INFERENCE OF STABLE FEATURES OF THE ENVIRONMENT

Kelley (1967) defines the domain of attribution theory in Heider's terms as the way in
which individuals interpret events as being
caused by stable parts of the environment. The
aim of the theory is to infer the dispositional
properties of entities in the environment. The
individual can choose to attribute the effects
of his actions either internally (to himself)
or externally (to the environment). Kelley
assumes that these effects are attributed to
conditions present when the effect takes place
or to conditions absent when the effect does
not take place. He suggests that a person examines four variations in respect to the observed action in order to determine internal
or external attribution of cause. These variations are examined to ascertain whether one's
impressions about an entity are due to dispositions of the entity and not to one's own idio-
syncrasies, or to one's interaction mode with
the entity. The four criteria of external
validity are:

1. *Distinctiveness.* An impression is attributed to
   an entity only if it occurs when the entity
   is present and if it does not occur in the
   entity's absence.
2. *Consistency over time.* During every instant in
   which the entity is present, the individual
   reacts to it in the same way.
3. *Consistency over modality.* Reactions to the
   entity are the same even when interaction
   modes vary (for example, one enjoys

reading the same book on a plane and at home).

4. *Consensus.* There is agreement and consistency on the part of others on how they experience the entity, which resembles that of the person's own experience.

Let us give an example. Suppose at work you are asked to read a report. When you are asked to react to it you find that you have enjoyed reading it tremendously. Does this suggest that your behavior is internally caused (you like this kind of report) or externally caused by the dispositions inherent to the report? If you enjoy reading this report (but not other reports or, at least, most others), if you enjoy reading it a second and third time, if you enjoy reading it at your office as well as at home, and if your colleagues also enjoy reading the report, then your reading enjoyment as an effect can be attributed to the report, the environmental entity. If these conditions are not met, you could make an attribution to yourself. Perhaps you have a submissive and easily persuasible disposition and a report suggested by a colleague is enjoyed because of these internal dispositions.

Kelley's observer is trying to rule out the error variance due to person properties in order to validly attribute an effect to stable parts of the environment. In the Jones and Davis (1965) model, the observer seeks variance in the situation caused by the person, and he tries to rule out situational variations of effects. This is why Jones and Davis deal with unique intentions rather than socially desirable behaviors. Socially desirable acts introduce situational consistencies and make attributions of personal causality difficult.

Kelley also lists some biases and errors that enter the process of attribution. These biases result in attributing personal cause when an external attribution should have been made or vice versa. One such bias results

when people ignore the relevant aspects of the
situation and make egocentric assumptions,
claiming to fulfill all four external validity
criteria when, in fact, only one is fulfilled
by the act. Consider a new supervisor taking
over a department. Chances are that if productivity increases, he will attribute the
success to his internal dispositions (such as
good leadership). If his workers fall below
standard levels of performance, he could attribute this decline to their dispositions of
laziness, lack of motivation, and so on. Another bias may result from the magnitude of
affective consequences in which attributions
are made for ego-protective reasons. Walster's
(1966) example suggested that strong affective
consequences result in the assignment of greater responsibility to actors. Finally, a person's perception of freedom and the unantici-
pated consequences of the action also bias the
attribution process. We shall discuss these two
conditions in the next chapter.

SOCIAL COMPARISON THEORY

People with whom we interact or whom we observe provide us with clues about the causes
of their behavior as well as of our own. By
comparing our behavior to that of others we can
infer whether the cause of our behavior is internal or is in response to a situation. In
discussing equity theory in chapter 3, we suggested that people have a drive to evaluate
their opinions and abilities in comparison to
those of meaningful others. These notions are
usually traced to Festinger's (1954) theory
of social comparison. Festinger posits that
one compares himself to others when objective
criteria for evaluating one's opinions and
abilities do not exist. Schacter (1959) has
applied the social comparison idea to his study
of how we label emotions. He argues that in
order to label our emotions, we account for
our reactions by observing what others are

feeling in the same situations. Kiesler (1978)
discusses this process of attribution, giving
experimental evidence for it.

ATTRIBUTION IN THE ORGANIZATIONAL CONTEXT

The behavior of people in organizations consists largely of their interacting with each
other. There are tasks on which joint work is
done, there are tasks one is ordered to do,
and tasks one orders others to do. Surveillance, trust, liking, ingratiation, ability,
responsibility, beliefs, attitudes, and emotions all come to play in the work place.
Correct attributions obviously lead to easier
interactions and more satisfactory work. However, we do not constantly try to infer the
dispositions of our supervisors, peers, and
subordinates in organizations. It would be
very time-consuming and a mental drain if,
while working in organizations, we were constantly preoccupied by inferring dispositions
through the complex steps delineated in the
models discussed in this chapter.

The variables of hedonic relevance and
personalism influence *when* we make attributions
in organizations. Other people in the organization may act in various ways. It is only when
we perceive that their behavior affects us
that we start making attributions. We can describe three situations in organizations where
an attributional analysis would be expected to
take place. One situation where a causality
attribution would occur is if people having
power over you become involved in a behavior
episode. Consider a supervisor who hires someone who has the same ability and specialty as
you. The question of why he hired the person
will occupy your mind. A second attribution-
causing situation occurs when an action comes
from an unexpected source. If the sales manager starts interviewing prospective candidates
for the accounting department of the organization, members of the accounting department will

be inferring various motives to his behavior. A third cause for attribution occurs when a person from whom a certain action is expected does not act. The sales manager who does not reply to letters from customers will be the subject of attributions. Frequently attributions made in organizational contexts are guided by a fear of being fired or a fear of losing control and power. Attributions made to others under conditions described above may lead to rumors and may be the basis for originating interpersonal conflicts. When there is no threat to our position in the organization, many behaviors by others go unnoticed. It is only when the behavior has hedonic relevance that we get involved in attribution.

REFERENCES

Bem, D. J. "Self-Perception: An Alternative Interpretation of Cognitive Dissonance Phenomena." *Psychological Review 24* (1967): 183-200.

Brunswick, E. *Perception and the Representative Design of Psychological Experiments*. 2nd ed. Berkeley, Calif.: Univ. of California Press, 1956.

DeCharms, R. *Personal Causation*. New York: Academic Press, 1968.

Festinger, L. "A Theory of Social Comparison Processes." *Human Relations 7* (1954): 117-40.

Heider, F. *The Psychology of Interpersonal Relations*. New York: Wiley, 1958.

Jones, E. E. *Ingratiation: A Social Psychological Analysis*. New York: Appleton-Century-Crofts, 1964.

Jones, E. E., and Davis, K. E. "From Acts to Dispositions: The Attribution Process in Person Perception." In *Advances in Experimental Social Psychology*, vol. 2, edited by L. Berkowitz, pp. 219-66. New York: Academic Press, 1965.

Jones, E. E.; Davis, K. E.; and Gergen, K. J. "Role Playing Variations and Their Informational Value for

Person Perception." *Journal of Abnormal Social Psychology 63* (1961): 302-10.

Jones, E. E., and DeCharms, R. "Changes in Social Perception as a Function of the Personal Relevance of Behavior." *Sociometry 20* (1957): 75-85.

Jones, E. E., and Harris, V. A. "The Attribution of Attitudes." *Journal of Experimental Social Psychology 3* (1967): 1-24.

Jones, E. E., and Nisbett, R. E. *The Actor and the Observer: Divergent Perceptions of the Causes of Behavior*. New York: General Learning Press, 1971.

Jones, E. E.; Rock, L.; Shaver, K. G.; Goethals, G. R.; and Ward, L. M. "Pattern of Performance and Ability Attribution: An Unexpected Primacy Effect." *Journal of Personality and Social Psychology 10* (1968): 317-40.

Kelley, H. H. "Attribution Theory in Social Psychology." In *Nebraska Symposium on Motivation*, edited by D. Levine. Lincoln, Nebraska: Univ. of Nebraska Press, 1967.

_____. *Attribution in Social Interaction*. New York: General Learning Press, 1971.

Kiesler, S. B. *Interpersonal Processes in Groups and Organizations*. Arlington Heights, Ill.: AHM Publishing Corporation, 1978.

Kruglanski, A. W. "Attributing Trustworthiness in Supervisor Worker Relations." *Journal of Experimental Social Psychology 6* (1970): 214-32.

Lanzetta, J. T., and Hannah, T. E. "Reinforcing Behavior of "Naïve" Trainers." *Journal of Personality and Social Psychology 11* (1969): 245-52.

Rothbart, M. "Effects of Motivation, Equity, and Compliance on the Use of Reward and Punishment." *Journal of Personality and Social Psychology 9* (1968): 353-62.

Rotter, J. B. "Generalized Expectancies for Internal Versus External Control of Reinforcement." *Psychological Monographs 80* (1966): 1-28.

Schacter, S. *The Psychology of Affiliation*. Stanford, Calif.: Stanford Univ. Press, 1959.

Storms, M. D. "Videotape and the Attribution Process: Reversing Actors' and Observers' Points of View." *Journal of Personality and Social Psychology 27* (1973): 165-75.

Strickland, L. H. "Surveillance and Trust." *Journal of Personality 26* (1958): 200-15.

Thibaut, J. W., and Riecken, H. W. "Some Determinants and Consequences of the Perception of Social Causality." *Journal of Personality 24* (1955): 113-33.

Walster, E. "Assignment of Responsibility for an Accident." *Journal of Personality and Social Psychology 3* (1966): 73-9.

Balance, Congruity, Dissonance

Balance, congruity, and dissonance are three different versions of a general cognitive consistency theory. All *cognitive consistency theories* share the notion that individuals behave in such a way as to minimize inconsistencies existing among their beliefs, cognitions, feelings, and behaviors. These theories posit a homeostatic motivational formulation which claims that inconsistency is an unpleasant state producing psychological discomfort and tension. The discomfort stimulates the individual to reduce inconsistency. The theories differ in their explanations of how consistency is established, but each tries to account for cognitive adjustments made by individuals in the process of attitude change.

We shall first discuss what gives rise to inconsistency in the cognitive apparatus of a person and the ways by which such inconsistency is reduced. Then we shall explain and evaluate

balance, congruity, and dissonance theories.
Table 7.1 summarizes the major constructs used
by each.

Discussion of these three theories raises
two important issues. The first is the definition of attitude. While each theory explains
the process of attitude change, they are all
referring to change in temporal attitudes—
those attitudes a person forms in response to
an immediate situation. Basically, these theories explain the change when the attitudes in
question are instantly formed in response to a
specific situation. Such attitudes are not
stable, enduring predispositions as were discussed in chapter 5. In this sense, the theories deal with a special case of attitudes.
Although this point is not elaborated it is
important for the reader to keep it in mind.
The second issue stems from the methods by
which the theories are tested. In the research
situation the subjects are pressured to maintain consistency. Furthermore, in order to
control the situation in the laboratory, most
avenues of inconsistency reduction are blocked
by the experimenter. This does not allow one
to observe how inconsistency is dealt with
naturally, when there is no pressure to change.
This issue will be raised in the section on
demand characteristics.

Cognitive consistency will emerge as a state
toward which the individual strives. However,
keep in mind that some motivation theories
posit a need for curiosity, arousal, and
complexity, as was discussed in chapter 3.
Individuals differ in the extent to which
they can tolerate inconsistency. Some of these
motivation theories may explain why persons
may actively maintain inconsistency.

It is important to emphasize that people in
organizations do not work in the tension-free
paradise that is the environment of cognitive
theories. Everyday living conditions may force
people to accept imbalanced states even if

TABLE 7.1 Important Variables in Cognitive Consistency Theories.

Theory	Major Constructs	Reduction of Inconsistency	Force Toward Change
Balance	Unit and sentiment relations between Person – Other – Object P – O – X	Change evaluation in the P-O-X triad	Stress due to imbalance
Congruity	Magnitude of attitude polarity between Source and Object	Change source and object attitudes	Symmetry
Dissonance	Number and magnitude of dissonant cognitions	Change attitude to bring it into consonance with the change in behavior with least effort possible	Psychological tension due to dissonance

they do not actively seek them. We seek competition and conflict in organizations. Nevertheless, it may be safe to assume that people also seek to simplify their world and balance their cognitions more often than they demand novelty and complexity.

INCONSISTENCY AND ITS REDUCTION

When a person enjoys his work and likes his boss, he has a consistent and usually pleasant relationship. However, scmetimes a person likes his job but dislikes his boss or vice versa. From time to time, all of us are faced with such inconsistencies. McGuire (1966) suggests several reasons why such inconsistencies exist. First, inconsistency can be due to human logical shortcomings (such as the ambiguous use of "some"). Cognitive consistency theories deal more with psychological shortcomings than with logical shortcomings. Second, inconsistency may arise because an individual occupies competing roles. A school official who is also a father may have to act in ways that are inconsistent with his father role. Third, a person's environment changes, leaving him with attitudes that no longer match reality. Politicians often find themselves in these situations. Fourth, an individual may experience external pressure to behave in ways inconsistent with his attitudes. Dissonance theorists have researched this situation. Finally, an individual may be influenced through exposure to new information and interpersonal interactions to espouse attitudes inconsistent with his previous beliefs.

When the cognitive apparatus has been disturbed by inconsistency, an attempt to forget the situation is an easy resolution. Forgetting is not always easy and a person has at his disposal several other ways to reduce inconsistency. One way is what Festinger (1957) calls *bolstering*. Here the person submerges the inconsistency in a large body of consistencies.

A related method is to show others their inconsistencies instead of facing one's own. A
more sophisticated approach is called *differentiation*. A person who finds that two of his cognitions are in conflict may try to differentiate
them. The individual who learns that his boss,
whom he hates, has donated a large sum of money
to his favorite charity may differentiate
between those aspects of his boss that he likes
and those he dislikes. We can briefly list some
other ways to reduce inconsistency: 1) down-
grading the importance of the source of the
inconsistency; 2) distorting perceptions; 3)
being selective in exposing oneself to information; 4) leaving the situation; 5) changing
one's attitude so that the inconsistency is
removed.

The alternatives to the reduction of inconsistency discussed above are all situation
dependent. We have to know the situation before
we even try to predict which alternative a person will choose. All of the above are ego-
defensive alternatives. By choosing any one
of them, the person protects his self-image
by being an honest, truthful, trustworthy,
decent sort of chap.

Sometimes we do not revert to any alternative
to reduce the inconsistency. Instead we simply
tolerate it. As technology spins a new image
of man, as everyday life becomes more complex,
and as information tends to become background
noise, we find ourselves as specialists of
small domains, tolerating more and more inconsistency in areas outside our fields of
expertise. The fact that human beings can
tolerate inconsistency does not invalidate the
general notion that inconsistency reduction
has reinforcing qualities. A structured, uni-
fied, consistent universe allows one to walk
in the world more securely, minimizes risk
inherent in new relationships, and brings
about pleasure due to predictability.

BALANCE THEORIES

HEIDER'S BALANCE THEORY

Heider (1958), credited with originating the balance notion, proposed a simple analysis to describe balance as a three-element system. Heider considers systems consisting of the person (P), another person (O), and an object (X). The elements of the system can have two types of relationships. *Sentiment relations* refer to affective feelings. P likes O, O likes X are sentiment relations. *Unit relations* encompass elements belonging together. Similarity, proximity, causality, common fate, membership, and ownership typify unit relations. P is O's father, P owns X are examples of unit relations. The three elements can have positive or negative relations between them. Heider considers a system balanced when the perceived units and experienced sentiments in the situation can co-exist without stress. Relations are always considered from P's vantage point. It is his perception that is important. Hence, a balanced relationship would be one where P likes O, P likes X, and P perceives O liking X. Most approaches study only the sentiment relations because they are not as ambiguous as unit relations. We could diagram possible three-element systems as Figure 7.1. Cartwright and Harary (1956) have formalized this model and their mathematical extensions suggest an easy formula for balance. Balance exists when the algebraic product of the signs is positive and does not exist when the product of the signs is negative.

Heider suggests that balance is a harmonious steady state, akin to homeostasis, and that individuals have a tendency to move toward this state. Balance states are stable and resistant to influence and change attempts. He argues that a halo-effect may be brought about by

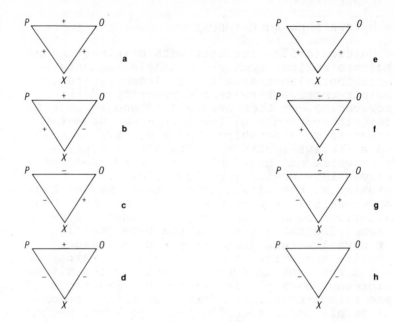

The triad is balanced when the algebraic product of
the signs is positive and imbalanced when the product
of the signs is negative.
SOURCE: F. Heider (1958).

FIGURE 7.1 Balanced and imbalanced states depicted by
relations among a person (P), another person (O), and
an object (X).

balance. The sentiment relation existing between P and O may generalize such that P comes
to hold positive all sentiments toward O,
creating a homogeneous system. A unit relation
such as P owns X may induce a sentiment relation, a liking for X.

States of imbalance produce stress and discomfort in the organism, leading to pressure
to change the system. If you like another person and also like football, but your friend
does not like football (triangle b, Figure

7.1), there exists imbalance in the system. *P*
will be under pressure to change the signs or
the relations in the system. Actually, there
are various alternatives for *P* in such a situation. You can decide not to like your friend
anymore (triangle *f*, Figure 7.1), or not to
like football (triangle *d*, Figure 7.1). Either alternative returns the system to balance.
However, *P* can differentiate between the
qualities of *O*, still maintaining balance in
the original system. *P* could say that *O* has
some likeable qualities and some bad characteristics, and it is *O*'s bad points that are
responsible for his not liking football. The
problem with Heider's approach is that he does
not specify which mode of imbalance resolution
a person will choose. He maintains, however,
that differentiation is a sophisticated way of
achieving balance, and that very few people
utilize this mode.

The three-element systems become somewhat
ambiguous when one tries to verbalize certain
possible situations. When there are three negative relations we have a state of imbalance
(triangle *h*, Figure 7.1). You dislike a coworker, and both of you dislike your boss. This
implies that there is a similarity between you
and your coworker, and hence, a positive unit
relation. This state moves toward balance when
this similarity is recognized, producing one
positive and two negative relations. Also, the
three positive relations can be imbalanced if
one considers a *menage à trois*. Dick loves Joan
and David, and Joan loves David. The potential
conflict in this situation is obvious even in
the most open society.

NEWCOMB'S VERSION OF BALANCE THEORY

Newcomb's theory is quite similar to
Heider's, even though it was developed as a
theory of interpersonal attraction and communication. According to Newcomb (1959), people
have psychological orientations towards others
(called *attractions*) and toward objects of

communication (called *attitudes*). A system of
orientation consists of two people (*A* and *B*)
and an object (*X*) and the judgments made by *A*
regarding *B*'s orientation towards *A* and *X*.
Newcomb suggests that we co-orient our perceptions when we meet others. We try to perceive
a person against the background of his attitudes. He states that there is a strain toward
symmetry (his concept of balance) in the system.
Communication is the major means for bringing
systems back into a state of symmetry. This
emphasis is absent in Heider's formulation.
Newcomb maintains that the strain toward symmetry is learned. Through their everyday relationships, people learn that communication
with others is easier when they hold similar
views. Communication is instrumental in reducing strain. When *A* finds out that a person
B, whom he likes, holds a view dissimilar to
his own about a certain object, the first attempt to regain symmetry is to communicate,
thereby trying to influence *B* to change his
views. This may allow for *B* to change, but
also exposes *A* to *B*'s attempts at influencing
him. If either *A* or *B* changes his views, symmetry can be obtained. Communication will not
always reduce symmetry; it may also increase
the strain. This depends to an extent on the
intensity of *A*'s attitude and his attraction
to *B*. It also depends on the relevance of
the attitude for both *A* and *B*. Disagreement
between *A* and *B* on coffee preference may not
be important for symmetry, but clashing values
may produce imbalance. If *A* does not trust *B*
very much and is highly committed to *X*, then
communication will not be likely to reduce
strain. *Imbalance* exists when the person perceives the relationship as such and tries to
move toward modification of the relations. If
the person is indifferent, uncertain, or
ambivalent, then a state of *nonbalance* exists.
Newcomb suggests that if *A* and *B* (*P* and *O* in
Heider) have a negative relation, there is
nonbalance.
The need for symmetry lies in a preference

for an ordered, consistent world and the desire
to avoid the anxiety that stems from conflict.
Symmetry leads to predictability of the person
with whom one interacts. Since attitudes are
shared, communication becomes easier. In this
case symmetry works as a secondary reinforcer.
Newcomb (1961) applied this theory to explain
how people get acquainted. His observation
of a group of total strangers starting to live
together showed that people adjusted their attitudes in order to maintain symmetry and to
attain mutual satisfaction.

EVALUATION OF BALANCE THEORIES

Both Heider and Newcomb maintain that balanced states are preferred over imbalanced
states. Research generally supports this notion. Jordan (1953) asked subjects to rate the
degree of pleasantness and unpleasantness of
hypothetical triadic sentiment and/or unit
relations. He found that, in general, balanced
states were rated as being more pleasant than
imbalanced states. In another study, Morisette
(1958) asked subjects to rate triadic situations involving themselves and two others, in
which all three would share an apartment. Subjects had to say how they would feel toward
one of their roommates based on given sentiment
relations. Balance theory predictions were that
if the subject was given two positive or two
negative sentiment relations, he would judge
the third relation as positive to maintain
balance. The results tended to agree with
these predictions. However, pleasantness and
stability are not always clearly related.
Price, Harburg, and Newcomb (1966) found that
only situations a and d in Figure 7.1 were
rated significantly pleasant, and situations
b , c , e , were rated significantly unpleasant. For situations f , g , and h the
ratings were split among pleasant, neutral,
and unpleasant in a nonsignificant way. The
way each subject reads the triad obviously
makes a difference even if the

triad is balanced in conceptual and algebraic terms.

Balance theory is simple and easily applicable to most phenomena, but neither Heider nor Newcomb has generated much research for his own theories. However, the balance notion, as identified by Heider, has influenced virtually all the variant cognitive consistency approaches. Most important, the theory has opened the way to considerable speculation and research on cognitive matters.

The simplicity of the theory in this case is also, perhaps, its weakness. Much of the theory rests on sentiment relations of the liking kind. However, liking is not defined, nor are the degrees of liking specified. Degrees of liking could be important. Intense liking or disliking could affect the amount of imbalance that a person would tolerate. Also, the cognitive system of an individual can produce differential tolerance rates for imbalance. Ability to fragment, to tolerate complexity, can lead a person to accept some imbalance as a way of life. Furthermore, the liking relation links people and objects without taking into account the affect associated with the object itself. Balance results only when liking is introduced to a triadic relationship.

The predictive power of the theory suffers because there is no statement regarding the means of imbalance reduction. When do people reach the detection threshold of imbalance, and how do they go about reducing imbalance? The researcher is in a bind trying to predict outcomes of situations. In their version of balance theory, Rosenberg and Abelson (1960) suggest that people will arrive at balance by choosing the route that requires the minimum effort. In addition, there is no mention of how balance is maintained among entities of differing natures. If you like your dog, and your dog likes dog food, you should also like dog food or else be subject to imbalance and stress. We leave it as an exercise to the reader to conceptualize ways by which a person can avoid imbalance without having to like dog food.

CONGRUITY THEORY

Congruity theory as developed by Osgood and Tannenbaum (1955), is in Heider's balance tradition and deals explicitly with attitude change due to communication. In this sense, the theory is more specific than Heider's and claims to make specific predictions in situations where a person has attitudes towards another person (called the source) and an object, and the source makes an evaluative statement about the object.

Osgood and Tannenbaum assert that people have a tendency toward maximum simplicity, that is, they tend to evaluate attitude objects as all good or as all bad. When two attitude objects become associated by an assertion, the theorists claim that there is a tendency for equilibrium or congruity. If two attitudes that differ in their evaluations are linked by an assertion, there will be a tendency for each attitude to shift to a new evaluation, which brings about congruity. Having congruent attitudes toward two related objects is simpler than maintaining different evaluations for each.

The assumptions made by this theory can best be illustrated by an example. Suppose a person has formed attitudes toward his boss and toward psychedelic drugs. Osgood and Tannenbaum measure his attitude with the *semantic differential* (described in chapter 5) by using the evaluative dimension only. This provides them with an attitude range from +3 to -3 for each item. Let us assume that our subject feels positive (+1) toward his boss and quite negative (-2) towards psychedelic drugs. Congruity comes into play when his two attitudes become linked. The boss makes a statement about psychedelic drugs. A source and an object can

be linked in a communicative message in an associative or a dissociative way; in other
words, the source can approve or disapprove of
the object. At an informal gathering, the boss
makes a statement indicating that he approves
of psychedelic drugs. At this point, the theory assumes that there will be pressure on the
person to bring his attitudes toward the boss
and psychedelic drugs into congruity. This
pressure is equal to the algebraic scale difference between the two objects. The sign is
positive when congruity is in the favorable
direction and negative when congruity is in
the unfavorable direction. The pressure that
exists when two attitudes are linked will
produce attitude change. This change will be
inversely proportional to the degree of polarization of the items. The objects of judgment
do not necessarily change equally. The more
polarized attitude changes less than the less
polarized attitudes. In this instance, we would
expect the person's attitude toward his boss
to change more than his attitude toward drugs.
In part (a) of Figure 7.2 the situation prior
to the statement is shown. Part (b) of Figure
7.2 shows how equilibrium is attained.

Congruity is obtained when a person feels
slightly negative toward both boss and drugs
at -1. The result of the statement has been to
make drugs a little less negative; but the
boss, to whom the less polarized attitude was
initially directed, has become negative whereas he was positive before the statement. This
kind of compromise is quite realistic. Instead of reverting to a single response which
modifies one attitude only, there may be more
psychological economy in slightly compromising
each attitude.

There are two points included here that
diverge from the previous theories. First,
the most important theoretical contribution is
the recognition that the person's attitudes
change toward both the source and the object.
According to balance theories, only one of
these attitudes would change. Second, the

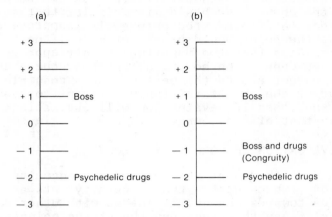

FIGURE 7.2 Example of attitude change as a result of an associative statement: (a) person's original positions, (b) congruity or equilibrium after assertion is made.

change is inverse to the degree of polarization. The polarity principle accounts for the fact that well established attitudes are more difficult to change.

Two other important points remain to be explained. When two highly divergent attitudes are linked by an assertion, they may not be believed. If a known communist praises the free market system, the tendency is to reject the statement as incredible coming from a communist. Osgood and Tannenbaum have empirically derived a formula to correct for such incredulity. Another empirically derived value is the *assertion constant*. The theory claims that attitudes toward both the source and the object change when they are brought together in a statement. Common sense suggests that the object attitude is more likely to change than the source attitude. For example, when Kissinger makes an assertion about Brezhnev, it is Brezhnev's evaluation that will change more. Having found this to be the case in their research, Osgood and Tannenbaum calculated an assertion constant which is a value added to the change and has a sign similar to the direction of predicted change. It seems to us that the point would be better made if one postulates that the magnitude of attitude change depends on how important the source and the object are to the person. It is possible that if the object is highly relevant to the person, then its evaluation will change less than that of the source.

EVALUATION OF CONGRUITY THEORY

One of the major assumptions of congruity theory, which states that congruity acts as a force towards change, is shared with other consistency theories. But the strong points of the theory can be found in its unique contributions to attitude change. The theory claims that: 1) both a source and an object are linked by an assertion change; and 2) the most polarized attitude object changes the least. These claims are further substantiated by mathematical statements that allow them to be tested.

Osgood and Tannenbaum (1955) tested the theory by first having subjects rate three sources and three concepts using the *semantic differential*. Five weeks later the subjects read newspaper accounts wherein the sources made favorable or unfavorable statements related to the concepts. After this, the subjects completed the *semantic differential* for a second time. When the before and after evaluations of the sources and the concepts were compared, the results fit well with the changes predicted by the theory.

In a sense, the theory satisfactorily explains certain tactics of politicians and advertisers. Keeping in mind that the most polarized object moves the least when linked to a less polarized object, we can see that the most effective play for an unknown politician is to praise those things that people evaluate positively while attacking unpopular objects. This immediately raises a candidate's credibility, at least as postulated by congruity theory. When a well known, likeable, attractive source (+3) links himself or herself to a new product (0) on television, the product has everything to gain. When Raquel Welch admires *Pit* deodorant, the expectation is that *Pit* will gain in favorability, while Raquel Welch remains as attractive as ever. Congruity can explain these phenomena, suggesting that, to the extent that the source is relevant to the person, incongruity is a disturbing state and a change is needed. The relevance notion is important. Kerrick (1958) found that if the source was relevant to the person, congruity theory predicted the attitude change more precisely than if the source was irrelevant. Remember, however, that balance theory can explain the same phenomenon, as can dissonance theory. Congruity theory makes the unique contribution of attempting to quantify the change that occurs based on the strength of prior evaluations, whereas balance theory deals with "all or nothing" positive and negative relationships.

Congruity theory also has some weaknesses. First, it is a limited theory that applies to certain communication studies and it has not been widely tested. Second, the theory suggests that the only way to restore congruity is through a change in prior evaluations of attitude objects as specified by the model. As we have seen in the introduction to this chapter, there are various ways of restoring balance. Osgood (1960) later agreed that congruity would also be achieved through various means such as bolstering and differentiation. Finally, there would be reason to believe that the degrees of positivity and intensity of an assertion would surely influence the evaluation of the attitude objects. The theory, unfortunately, does not define and describe assertions.

COGNITIVE DISSONANCE THEORY

The theory of cognitive dissonance initially elaborated by Festinger (1957) has been the most researched cognitive consistency theory. The reason for this might be found in some of the nonobvious but intriguing predictions made by the theory. It has been tested in many cognitive-motivational areas, and although this book is not the place to summarize its many findings and controversies, we shall describe the major postulates of the theory, and then show how it has evolved over the years.

Festinger, like other consistency theorists, begins by positing that balance and harmony among cognitions is a desired state. The absence of balance and harmony creates tensions within the organism that motivate the person to establish consistency. If we abstract two cognitions from the complex of all cognitions embedded in the organism, we can formalize three possible kinds of relationships between these cognitions: irrelevant, consonant, and dissonant. In the first case, the cognitions have nothing to do with each other; they are *irrelevant* to one another. "I like women with long hair" and "It is snowing in Kilimanjaro" are irrelevant cognitions. In the second case, cognitions follow each other; they are consistent, therefore they have a *consonant* relationship. "I like women with long hair" and "I am married to a woman with long hair" is a consonant relationship. In the third case, cognitions may not follow each other such that one cognition implies the opposite of the other; then, they are in a *dissonant* relationship. "An affinity for hot weather" and "living in Northern Canada" are in a dissonant relationship. The second cognition does not follow from the first. The first cognition implies the opposite of the second one. Dissonant relationships can occur because of logical inconsistency, cultural mores, past experience, and so on. The psychological consistency or inconsistency between cognitions may be more

important than the logical consistency or inconsistency when one is attempting to understand behavior.

The theory makes two assumptions related to
cognitions in a dissonant relationship. The
first assumption is that dissonance creates
psychological tension which motivates the
person to make his cognitions consonant. A
second assumption is that people tend to avoid
dissonance and that if dissonance exists they
will try to avoid certain kinds of situations
and information that would increase it.

MAGNITUDE OF DISSONANCE

It is obvious that many cognitions can be
dissonant and that people can tolerate dissonance. For instance, to use Festinger's
classic example, smoking cigarettes and the
knowledge that they cause cancer are dissonant
cognitions. However, many people go on smoking.
This suggests that there is a tolerance threshold for dissonance. The motivational effects
of dissonance depend on its magnitude. The
magnitude of dissonance will be higher the
greater the number and importance of the
elements in the relationship. A person in debt
will experience more dissonance if he buys a
new car than if he gives some money to a
beggar; the more reasons known to a person for
stopping smoking, the more dissonance he should
experience if he continues to smoke.

DISSONANCE AND MOTIVATION

Dissonance creates a state of discomfort in
the organism which has motivational effects.
Although never explicitly stated, dissonance is
conceived as a drive state which activates and
directs the organism to reduce psychological
cognitive discomfort aroused by inconsistency.
In chapter 3 we suggested that if someone's
motive is blocked before he reaches a goal,
frustration, which is a new motivational
state, takes place. Dissonance is usually

associated with the goal. In organizations,
we can conceive of goals as having positive
and negative attributes. The choice of a goal
is a decision made by an individual who is
constantly choosing among goals involving
attractive and unattractive attributes. A
person experiences conflict before choosing
among alternatives, but once a choice is made,
dissonance may exist if the person discovers
that he has not made the best choice. The
theory postulates that when people make a
choice they will try to minimize dissonance by
avoiding information about the goal that was
not chosen and seeking information about the
preferred goal. The reduction of dissonance
in goal conflicts is important in minimizing
postdecision regret for the unchosen alternative.

   There are three types of goal conflicts:
approach-approach, approach-avoidance, and
avoidance-avoidance conflicts. In an *approach-
approach* type of conflict, the person has to
choose between two positive goals relatively
similar in their attractiveness. A person
offered a choice of two different promotions,
or two different offices can experience post-
decision conflict due to dissonance. *Approach-
avoidance* conflicts are those typical of organizations in which a goal is seen to have positive and negative attributes. A project has
many approach tendencies, but the negative
aspects become more evident as more energy and
money need to be committed to reach the goal.
Many times a choice must be made in terms of
approaching or avoiding the goal: the committee
in charge of the project will have to decide
to carry it through or to shelve it. These
choices too, can create postdecision dissonance. *Avoidance-avoidance* type of conflicts
describe a choice between two equally unattractive goals. These conflicts are usually
resolved by a person's either leaving the situation or avoiding decision-making. Tuggle
(1978) discusses various goal conflicts in
organizations.

Other things being equal, dissonance depends
upon how important the decision is and how
initially attractive is the unchosen alternative. In a situation where a person is free
to choose among alternatives, dissonance can
be reduced by revoking the decision or by increasing the attractiveness of the chosen
alternative and decreasing the attractiveness
of the unchosen one. Research suggests that
people follow the latter options because a
choice is usually an episode of public behavior
and would be very difficult to revoke. Brehm
(1956) found that his subjects increased the
attractiveness of a product they chose and
decreased the attractiveness of an unchosen
product. Both products were of equal attractiveness before the choice. Ehrlich et al.
(1957) tried to assess the attitudes of new
car owners. They hypothesized that people who
had recently bought a new car would look at
advertisements about their make of car and
ignore advertisements about other makes they
had considered buying. Their data supported
their predictions. You can see that here,
basically, is a process of selective exposure
wherein people seek supportive information and
avoid disconfirming information. This finding
has not been supported by subsequent studies.

DISSONANCE AND ATTITUDE CHANGE

When a person chooses to act in a certain
manner, he cannot reduce ensuing dissonance
by negating his behavior. The choice to act
commits the person, and the act itself becomes
public. The person can, as we have already
suggested, change his cognitions, thereby
bringing them into consistency with his actions. It is in this domain that dissonance
makes some nonobvious predictions. Let us look
at a typical study to try to understand the
process.

Festinger and Carlsmith (1959) had their
subjects spend about an hour turning pegs on
a board. When it was over, the extremely boring

task was described to the subjects as a test
of the effect of expectancy on performance.
The experimenter explained that some subjects
had been told beforehand that they were going
to do a very interesting task. Then, on the
excuse that his assistant was absent, the experimenter asked the subjects who had completed
the task to meet the next subject and tell him
that the task was very interesting. The subjects were also told that they would be on call
for this routine in the future and were offered
$1 or $20. Most of the subjects agreed to tell
someone else that what actually was a very dull
task was very interesting. Of interest was the
subjects' attitudes about the task after tell-
ing others that the task was interesting. Subjects paid $1 thought that the task was less
boring than those who were paid $20. How can
we explain this intriguing result? The highly
rewarded subjects reduced dissonance by thinking that they performed a dull task but were
well paid to help the experimenter by lying
about it. They could continue to think that
the task was dull and maintain consistency,
whereas subjects in the low-reward condition
did not have enough justification to say the
task was interesting. To reduce dissonance,
they came to believe what they said. This situation in which a person is induced to act in
opposition to his beliefs is known as forced
compliance. Note that the finding is nonobvious. A simple reinforcement view would have
predicted that the $20 subjects would think
the task was interesting.

Typical approaches to the study of attitude
change suggest that attitudes affect behavior and therefore, if one changes attitudes
an ensuing behavioral change may be produced.
Dissonance theory, as the experiment described
above demonstrates, espouses the opposite
viewpoint. A behavior is changed in order to
obtain attitude change. Three important aspects have to be considered when expecting
an attitude change to result from a behavior
change. These are *volition*, *prior commitment*, and

relevance of task. If someone has volition (that
is, if he is free to choose) dissonance will
exist if he does something contrary to his attitudes. If the individual has no choice but
to perform the contrary behavior, there is
no need to reduce dissonance and change his
attitudes. Hence, the more pressure exerted on
a person to behave contrary to his attitudes,
the less need to reduce dissonance. Equally
important is the degree of public commitment.
If the degree is high, the behavior then becomes irrevocable. Finally, whether or not the
behavior is public and whether or not there is
volition, it is important that an individual
think that his task was relevant. Trivial behaviors in which compliance was obtained contrary to prior attitudes may not produce dissonance.

THE EFFECTS OF REWARDS ON ATTITUDES AND BEHAVIOR

In the Festinger and Carlsmith (1959) study
just described, subjects who were paid less
to call a dull task interesting came to believe
what they were saying, whereas those who were
paid more did not change their beliefs. This
finding, which has been replicated in various
situations by other dissonance theorists (see
Brehm and Cohen, 1962) runs counter to a
general reinforcement principle. As discussed
in chapter 1, a learning approach suggests that
people tend to evaluate positively behaviors
that are rewarded. A person will involve himself in self-persuasion geared toward changing
his attitudes when offered a reward for
counterattitudinal behavior. Dissonance theorists do not disagree with this notion. They
claim, however, that this tendency may reverse
itself in some situations which they carefully
try to specify. Consequently, most of the effort by theorists and experimenters is concentrated on the problem of specifying the
conditions under which rewards have dissonance
effects and incentive effects. "Dissonance,"

"commitment," and "incentive" are three theoretical approaches dealing with the effects
that rewards and incentives have on attitude
change.

Dissonance theory examines how a person
reacts when he has been paid for a counterattitudinal act. Dissonance research suggests
that subjects who are paid a smaller amount
become more favorable toward the counterattitudinal act than those who are paid more.
Commitment theorists study the effects of rewarding a consonant act. For example, suppose
that people committed to an attitude are
paid a small amount to first perform a consonant act. They will resist an attack on the
attitude more than members of another group,
also committed to the attitude, who have been
paid more (Kiesler, 1971). Taken together,
commitment and dissonance theories suggest
that large incentives will have a less effect
than smaller incentives. That is, those who
act against their beliefs change less and
those who act with their beliefs are less
resistant to attack.

Whereas dissonance theory predicts that
small payments generate greater dissonance and
greater attitude shifts than large ones (which
themselves provide sufficient justification for
the counterattitudinal behavior), incentive
theory posits that large payments can make
people more inclined to "biased scanning" and
result in larger attitude shifts (Elms, 1967).
In trying to resolve the debate, Linder,
Cooper, and Jones (1967) found that the time
when the reward is given is crucial in understanding the relationship between the magnitude of money and the degree of attitude
change. If the money is given before the
counterattitudinal act (before commitment),
it is an "incentive." The larger the incentive,
the less attitude change is to be expected
(dissonance theory explanation). If the money
is given after the person commits himself to
an act, it is a "reward" and the larger the reward
the more attitude change should be expected

(incentive theory explanation). Clearly, their work relies on how a person interprets the meaning of the money. Steiner (1972) tried to solve the controversy from that perspective. If the incentive is offered before commitment with a choice to decline it, then it may be seen as a bribe. If the incentive is interpreted as a bribe, then the larger the incentive offered, the less will be the attitude change (dissonance theory). If a reward is given after commitment with no choice to decline it, the reward will be seen as a gold star. If the money is perceived as a gold star, then the larger the payment offered, the greater will be the attitude change (incentive theory).

One way of interpreting this difference is the "insufficient justification" hypothesis. When a person receives money for acting and thus has ample justification for his behavior, he need not attribute his behavior to his own beliefs. But when he does not expect external rewards, or he expects only minimal rewards, he must attribute his behavior to his own beliefs.

We can ask whether, as incentive theory predicts, large payments, received after one acts, always result in further attitude change. There are some who believe that too large, or overly sufficient rewards will not bolster, but rather will undermine belief; that is, the person will reflect on his act and think, "Well, maybe if one has to be paid to perform an act, it is not worth so much to me." Nisbett and Valins (1971) suggest that large rewards given after an act may have a negative effect. The reason is related to the implication a large reward can have for one's own motivation to act in the first place. Therefore, one should, in studying rewards and attitude change in free choice situations, look at initial motivation to act. The reader is referred to the discussion on intrinsic and extrinsic motivation in chapter 3 for further points.

DISSONANCE AND SELF-PERCEPTION

Bem (1967) has offered a different explanation of dissonance phenomena. He argues that what has been labeled dissonance is the individual's inferences about the causes of his own behavior, thus explaining dissonance from an attribution point of view. The explanation is based on his theory of attitude formation. According to Bem, behaviors cause attitudes. A person forms attitudes through a process of self-perception. If someone questions how you feel about your work, you reason "I go to work, therefore I must like my work." Your reply, accordingly, is that you like your work. This is a process very similar to the one in which a person attributes causality to others. You observe people's behavior to get a clue about their internal states.

Bem's interpretation of the forced compliance studies is also based on self-perception and attribution. He explains the predictions of the Festinger and Carlsmith experiment in the same way as he explains dissonance theory. The person who receives $1 decides that he does not have enough justification to lie. In Bem's words, his behavior is tacted, whereas the behavior of the $20 subject is manded. It is under the control of external sources. Individuals do not change their attitudes and beliefs if their behavior is manded. The difference between Bem's approach and dissonance theory is that Bem explains dissonance as temporal attitudes based on acts, whereas the latter theory expounds its tenets on the notion of cognitive consistency.

Bem has tested his approach by describing to his subjects the conditions of the Festinger and Carlsmith study and asking them to predict how the subjects in the experiment would feel at the end of it. His subjects were able to replicate the results. Bem suggests that his subjects infer the internal states of the subjects in the experiment from their behavior in the experiment, and that those subjects who were in the experiment do the same with their own behaviors and attitudes. In other words, an internal drive state called dissonance is not experienced; rather, actions are interpreted. A simpler explanation of Bem's data might be that observers can predict behavior accurately in dissonance situations.

Tedeschi et al. (1971) extend Bem's approach, suggesting that what happens in dissonance experiments is an effort on the part of subjects to control the impressions formed about them by the experimenter. For example, many subjects prefer to think of themselves as reasonable and fair. If they are paid and asked to behave inconsistently with this self image, the payment and the request by the experimenter are seen as mands. Hence, because their behavior was manded, they usually will not make any attempt to adjust their cognitions to fit their manded behaviors. It is crucial for the observer to see mand qualities in the behaviors. It is only when two incompatible behaviors appear to the observers to be tacted that the person will make an effort to change.

DEMAND CHARACTERISTICS IN EXPERIMENTAL SITUATIONS

A potentially serious source of bias exists in laboratory studies. Even though every situation makes demands on people to act or behave in certain ways, social laboratories are compelling settings. Subjects in laboratory studies exemplify demand characteristics (Orne, 1962, 1969). In their quest to be good subjects and to further science, they may approach the experimental task as a problem to be solved in such a way that by acting correctly they will provide the "right" data for the experimenter. Orne details this phenomenon saying it cannot be eliminated, but care can be taken to measure its effect on an experiment's outcome.

Rosenberg (1965) suggests that a condition

he calls *evaluation apprehension* contaminates the results of dissonance experiments. He defines evaluation apprehension as the subjects' search for hypotheses that will bring them positive evaluations and help them avoid negative evaluations. Rosenberg claims that the subjects in the $20 condition of the Festinger and Carlsmith study feel that their honesty is measured and so they do not change their attitudes. Ellsworth (1966) interviewed her subjects after a dissonance experiment and found that 15% of them responded to demand characteristics, 37% to evaluation apprehension, and 28% gave dissonance reduction as the reason for their actions. We believe that both Bem and Tedeschi et al. may be criticizing the demand characteristic aspect of dissonance theory and putting the findings in an alternative perspective. The kind of guessing that subjects do may have also been operating in congruity and balance experiments.

Another valuable suggestion is made by Aronson (1969) in his reformulation of dissonance theory. For him, dissonance reduction serves as ego-defensive behavior, helping an individual maintain a positive self-image. A person will reduce dissonance only if his self-image can be protected. When his integrity, his self-image, is threatend by his having acted in a certain way, an individual will try to make up for it by changing his attitudes. Thus, lying to someone for $1 is dissonant with a self-image that is decent, truthful, and trustworthy. So the individual comes to believe what he says to protect his integrity.

EVALUATION OF COGNITIVE DISSONANCE THEORY

While explaining dissonance theory we evaluated various aspects of it which we shall briefly summarize now. From its inception, cognitive dissonance theory has generated an abundance of studies on a scale rarely seen in the social and psychological arena. This theory continues to generate research that is now more geared toward limiting its boundary conditions. Even so, the theory can be subjected to some valid criticism.

In most studies, dissonance is an assumed state. The experimenters create a situation where they hope subjects will feel dissonance. However, since it is an intervening variable, dissonance is never measured. Some dissonance results are open to various alternative explanations which are difficult to rule out. In the posttest to measure attitudes, subjects who do not conform to the experimenter's prior demands to act in certain ways are left out of studies. In free choice studies, subjects who decide to choose an unpreferred alternative over an initially preferred one are also discarded from the study. Subject loss of this nature creates serious problems in generalization. Frequently researchers construct experiments so that they reduce dissonance by leaving the subjects only one avenue. In actuality, various modes of dissonance reduction exist and it would be interesting to find how people will reduce dissonance when all avenues are open to them. This will open the way to the study of individual differences in dissonance reduction. The importance of the cognitive elements and the resistance to change of cognitions have not been measured. Many of the theory's concepts remain vague, including the definition of dissonance itself.

REFERENCES

Aronson, E. "The Theory of Cognitive Dissonance: A Current Perspective." In *Advances in Experimental Social Psychology*, vol. 4, edited by L. Berkowitz, pp. 1-34. New York: Academic Press, 1969.

Bem, D. J. "Self-Perception: An Alternative Interpretation of Cognitive Dissonance Phenomena." *Psychological Review 74* (1967): 183-200.

Brehm, J. W. "Post-Decision Changes in the Desirability of Alternatives." *Journal of Abnormal and Social Psychology 52* (1956): 384–89.

Brehm, J. W., and Cohen, A. R. *Explorations in Cognitive Dissonance.* New York: Wiley, 1962.

Cartwright, D., and Harary, F. "Structural Balance: A Generalization of Heider's Theory." *Psychological Review 63* (1956): 277–93.

Ehrlich, D.; Guttman, I.; Schonbach, P; and Mills, J. "Post-Decision Exposure to Relevant Information." *Journal of Abnormal and Social Psychology 54* (1957): 98–102.

Ellsworth, P. "Dissonance Reduction from the Subject's Point of View." *American Psychologist 21* (1966): 684.

Elms, A. C. "Role Playing, Incentive, and Dissonance." *Psychological Bulletin 68* (1967): 132–48.

Festinger, L. *A Theory of Cognitive Dissonance.* Stanford, Calif.: Stanford University Press, 1957.

Festinger, L., and Carlsmith, J. M. "Cognitive Consequences of Forced Compliance." *Journal of Abnormal and Social Psychology 28* (1959): 203–10.

Heider, F. *The Psychology of Interpersonal Relations.* New York: Wiley, 1958.

Jordan, N. "Behavioral Forces That Are a Function of Attitudes and Cognitive Organization." *Human Relations 6* (1953): 273–87.

Kerrick, J. "The Effect of Relevant and Nonrelevant Sources on Attitude Change." *Journal of Social Psychology 47* (1958): 15–20.

Kiesler, C. A. *The Psychology of Commitment.* New York: Academic Press, 1971.

Linder, D. E.; Cooper, J.; and Jones, E. E. "Decision Freedom as a Determinant of the Role of Incentive Magnitude in Attitude Change." *Journal of Personality and Social Psychology 5* (1967): 245–54.

McGuire, W. J. "The Current Status of Cognitive Consistency Theories." In *Cognitive Consistency: Motivational Antecedents and Behavioral Consequents,* edited by S. Feldman, pp. 1-46. New York: Academic Press, 1966.

Morisette, J. "An Experimental Study of the Theory of Structural Balance." *Human Relations 11* (1958): 239-54.

Newcomb, T. M. "Individual Systems of Orientation." In *Psychology: A Study of a Science*, vol. 3, edited by E. Koch, pp. 384-422. New York: McGraw-Hill, 1959.

_____. *The Acquaintanceship Process*. New York: Holt, Rinehart and Winston, 1961.

Nisbett, R. E., and Valins, S. *Perceiving the Causes of One's Behavior*. New York: General Learning Press, 1971.

Orne, M. T. "On the Social Psychology of the Psychological Experiment: With Particular Reference to Demand Characteristics and Their Implications." *American Psychologist 17* (1962): 776-83.

_____. "Demand Characteristics and the Concept of Quasi-Controls." In *Artifact in Behavioral Research*, edited by R. Rosenthal and R. L. Rosnow, pp. 143-79. New York: Academic Press, 1969.

Osgood, E. C. "Cognitive Dynamics in the Conduct of Human Affairs." *Public Opinion Quarterly 24* (1960): 341-65.

Osgood, E. C., and Tannenbaum, P. H. "The Principle of Congruity in the Prediction of Attitude Change." *Psychological Review 65* (1955): 42-55.

Price, K.; Harburg, E.; and Newcomb, T. "Psychological Balance in Situations of Negative Interpersonal Attitudes." *Journal of Personality and Social Psychology 3* (1966): 265-70.

Rosenberg, M. J. "When Dissonance Fails: On Eliminating Evaluation Apprehension from Attitude Measurement." *Journal of Personality and Social Psychology 1* (1965): 28-42.

Rosenberg, M., and Abelson, R. "An Analysis of Cognitive Balancing." In *Attitude Organization and Change*, edited by C. Hovland and M. Rosenberg, pp. 112-63. New Haven, Conn: Yale University Press, 1960.

Steiner, I. D. "Perceived Freedom." In *Advances in Experimental Social Psychology*, vol. 5, edited by L. Berkowitz. New York: Academic Press, 1972.

Tedeschi, J. T.; Schlenker, B. R.; and Bonoma, T. V. "Cognitive Dissonance: Private Ratiocination or Public Spectacle?" *American Psychologist 26* (1971): 685–95.

Tuggle, F. D. *Organizational Processes*. Arlington Heights, Ill.: AHM Publishing Corporation, 1978.

Personality

Personality may be defined as a stable set of characteristics which describe the psychological processes and behavior of people. Because the word has lost most of its denotative and connotative meaning, it is helpful to examine personality by describing what *personologists* (those interested in the study of personality) do. Personologists are interested in the whole person as a unit of study. Maddi (1972) defines their concern as the study of groups of people to find how these samples are representative of people in general. Inherent in this attempt to discover commonalities is the effort to discover individual differences. Personality is usually not studied in terms of a behavior observed at a given moment. Rather, behavior is generally traced to its social and biological roots. The reason for this approach is the belief held by most personologists that human behavior is complex, and that personality is extremely resistant to change.

Personologists also believe that personality comes to full bloom in adulthood; consequently the subject pool for the study of personality is adult human beings.

This chapter will give an overview of personality theories. The selective sampling of the vast literature will start with the description of theoretical approaches to the study of personality. It will be seen that most theories stress the importance that development from childhood to adulthood plays in shaping personality. We shall review both developmental stages identified by different theorists and the biological and environmental determinants of personality. We shall point to the *self* as the core tendency of personality. Finally, we shall briefly look at some frequently studied personality *traits*, which are the enduring aspects of the personality, both stable and manifested in various situations. Problems related to the measurement of traits will be identified.

The focus of study in personality is the normal, healthy adult individual. Abnormal behavior and maladjusted individuals are also studied to determine what divergence exists between normalcy and maladjustment. The aim is to understand how the various characteristics of the person add up to form a whole individual who has a unique personality structure. The search for these structures results in categorizing behaviors into systems which allow economy of explanation for the immense diversity that exists in behavior. However, we shall argue that research on personality traits has failed in predicting behavior across situations. Part of this fault involves methodological problems due to measurement techniques; part also lies in insufficient sampling of situations when studying personality.

THEORIES OF PERSONALITY

Personologists have expended a great deal of

effort in suggesting theories that explain the whole human being. Most of these theories claim to be broad, encompassing all human be- haviors. Others claim to explain only specific behaviors. Since a thorough review of all personality theories is beyond the scope of this chapter, we have selected a few in order to give you an appreciation of personality theories.[1] We shall review psychoanalytic theory as exemplified by Freud's work, trait theories, and humanistic approaches.

PSYCHOANALYTIC THEORY

Psychoanalytic theory was developed by Sigmund Freud at the turn of the century (see Freud, 1953). Everyone who considers himself to be a lay psychologist will have something to say about Freud. His contribution to personality theory, although often misunder- stood, is both historically and conceptually important.

Freud was convinced that motivation was the key to understanding people. He felt that an individual's personality is firmly grounded in childhood experiences. Hence an individual's responses to his environment are based on his past learning and motivations. Consequently, he believed that most human motives are sub- merged in the unconscious, and that many of our behaviors are guided by repressed feelings and unconscious motives from our childhood past. Understanding how behavior was caused means determining what these unconscious motives are. Freud's observations were based to a large extent on neurotic persons, and because of this approach many people now feel that his theory is applicable only to the maladjusted.

Freud conceived of personality as being compartmentalized into three structures; the id, the ego, and the superego. The *id* was described as the animal part of every human being, operating on the pleasure principle. It seeks to obtain immediate gratification by satisfying instincts and impulses. The

ego is the balancing force, aiming at pre-
serving the individual. It functions on the
reality principle, testing reality and occasionally fighting off the demands of the id.
The ego is our external representation. The
superego functions on moral grounds, internaliz-
ing parental and societal values and acting as
a mirror of our socialization. The superego
judges right and wrong, good and bad.

   This tripartite system, according to Freud,
is in constant conflict. Since the id and
superego make different motivational demands,
they must be tempered by the ego. The id makes
demands on the ego which the ego does not
gratify; the superego is at odds both with the
id and the ego since they cannot meet its
moral code. The result of this conflict between the structures is anxiety, which results
in tension, which in turn must be reduced.
If the organism cannot reduce this tension
realistically, it resorts to defenses. The
notion of *defensive mechanisms* is an important
contribution of psychoanalytic theory. Freud
saw defensive mechanisms as a response of the
ego to excessive pressure. The mechanisms were
characterized as falsifying reality and
operating at the level of the unconscious. It
is commonly accepted today that most defense
mechanisms are helpful in situations involving
pressure, and unless they are continuously used
help many individuals to adjust to difficult
situations.

DEFENSIVE BEHAVIORS IN ORGANIZATIONS. Defensive
behaviors have motivational undertones. Conflicts and their ensuing anxiety and pressure
arise when goal-directed behavior is blocked.
A typical response to frustration generated
because of goal-blockage is to engage in
defensive behaviors. One of the most typical
responses to frustration is aggression. Psychoanalytic theory has uncovered some other important defensive behaviors which are reviewed
below:

DISPLACEMENT. When the source causing the anxiety cannot be attacked, energy is displaced on an appropriate target. The employee who was frustrated by his boss can displace his emotions on another worker or on his wife.

PROJECTION. This occurs when the anxiety is caused by one's own impulses and inhibitions. To protect himself, the person attributes his own feelings to someone else. Instead of "I hate the boss" one can say "the boss hates me."

RATIONALIZATION. Perhaps the most commonly used of defensive behaviors, rationalization requires justifying one's own undesirable behavior by providing acceptable explanations. Blaming equipment failure for one's bad performance; or, after an expected promotion falls through, making the claim that one did not want the responsibility anyway are two examples of rationalization.

REPRESSION. In Freudian terms this is the denial of conflict. The person represses to the unconscious that with which he cannot cope. Many unpleasant situations on the job are repressed.

REGRESSION. Anxiety is sometimes dealt with by reverting to infantile forms of behavior. This temporary regression to childlike behavior alleviates the tension. Horseplay is one form of regression; becoming involved in doing what the subordinates should do is another.

REACTION-FORMATION. Similar to projection, an impulse or feeling which is difficult to accept and which causes conflict is repressed and its opposite is espoused. Feelings of hate may be replaced with love. Disappointment over the loss of a promotion might be repressed and the company praised.

WITHDRAWAL. Avoiding reality is one way to deal with anxiety. Daydreaming, fantasizing, and flight are all withdrawal symptoms. Boring jobs lead to withdrawal. Absenteeism is many times a manifest form of withdrawal.

Defensive mechanisms are not constructive ways by which to deal with anxiety. But they accomplish what the term signifies: they

temporarily protect the individual against an
unfriendly external environment. Most of us
make use of defensive mechanisms. It is only
when they dominate behavior that they become
counteradaptive. This signifies that the ego
has not been able to manage the conflict, and
the result is a psychologically sick person.

TYPE AND TRAIT THEORIES

Various personality theorists have approached
the problem of theorizing by devising taxono-
mies to aid in classifying people. Two such
approaches are type and trait theories. Type
theories approach personality by sorting
people into discrete categories, or types.
This approach was considered by Sheldon (1940),
who proposed three body types and tried to
establish relationships between body types
and temperament. He found that endomorphic
people were sociable, mesomorphic people were
energetic, and ectomorphic people were sensitive loners. His type theory has not been
very popular. Jung (1923) a former colleague
of Freud, also proposed a type theory, based
on psychological factors. He considered all
people to be either introverts or extroverts.
Introverts were characterized as shy loners,
keeping their feelings and emotions to themselves. Extroverts were outgoing, sociable,
involved in interpersonal relationships. Most
people at the managerial level in organizations would be classified as extroverts.
Utilizing psychoanalytical research techniques, Maccoby (1976) has identified four
types of managerial personality, which he calls
i) the craftsman, ii) the jungle fighter,
iii) the company man, and iv) the gamesman,
respectively. These types were derived by
analyzing extensive interviews with top and
middle level managers of several leading
companies. The interviews included responses
to projective tests and descriptions of the
executives' dreams.

The four managerial types that Maccoby identified can be briefly described as:

i) *The Craftsman*. The craftsman's values are
related to the work-ethic. He respects people,
has concern for quality of products and tends
to be thrifty. He is the perfectionist type
who has difficulty leading a large and ever
changing organization. Scientists working in
organizations are a good example of this type.
Craftsmen do not necessarily share the values
of the organization in which they work.
Rather, they see organizations as places where
they can work on interesting jobs and pursue
their creations. Some craftsmen are receptive
and democratic; others are authoritarian and
intolerant.

ii) *The Jungle Fighter*. The goal for the jungle
fighter is power. He perceives his peers
either as accomplices or enemies. Subordinates
are viewed as objects to be utilized. There
are two types of jungle fighters: a) the lions
who, when successful build empires (e.g.,
Andrew Carnegie); and, b) the foxes who sur-
vive within the corporate hierarchy and move
ahead by politicking. In its classical view
an entrepreneur would be a good example of a
jungle fighter.

iii) *The Company Man*. This type is similar to
Whyte's (1956) notion of the organization man
who takes solace in being part of a powerful
and protective company. The company man is
interested in the feelings of those around
him and is committed to maintain the organization's integrity.

iv) *The Gamesman*. The gamesman emerged from
the study as the successful managerial type of
our days. His interests are in challenge and
competitive activity where he can prove himself to be a winner. The gamesman responds
to work and life as a game. He takes moderate
risks, likes new ideas and techniques. He
motivates and pushes others he works with to
their limits. His main goal in life is to be a
winner.

Maccoby suggests that the gamesman type more
often than any other managerial type that
he studied occupies the higher echelons of the
organization. He feels that successful managers
in modern day organizations are those that
combine characteristics of the gamesman and
the company man.

A problem inherent in typologies is the expectation that, once a person has been classified, many assertions can be made about him.
This can lead to unnecessary stereotyping.
Type theories also rely heavily on biological
determination of personality at the expense
of neglecting the role played by cultural
factors and socialization.

Whereas typologists divide people discretely
in a category, *trait theorists* assume a continuous dimension on which people can be quanti-
tatively arranged according to how much of the
dimension they exhibit. Traits such as ag-
gressiveness, achievement, and dominance have
been studied to see how people differ on these
dispositions. Allport (1937) was a prominent
trait theorist. He believed that each individual is unique. But, because of their
shared experiences, people also display some
common traits that can be studied. The Allport
scale of values (Allport et al., 1960) was
devised to distinguish common traits related
to preferred theoretical, economic, esthetic,
social, political, and religious values. The
emphasis was, nevertheless, on uniqueness with
the aim of understanding cardinal, central,
and secondary traits. *Cardinal traits* are those
that seem to guide the life of an individual.
Central traits are dispositions that are sufficient to characterize the person. *Secondary traits*
are the dispositions or attitudes the person
develops. Personality, according to Allport,
can be best understood by studying the structure of those dispositions which display a
somewhat organized hierarchy.

Cattell (1965), another well known trait
theorist, started with a comprehensive list of
words denoting personality traits. Using

factor analytical techniques he collapsed these traits into surface and source traits. *Surface traits* are clusters of overt dimensions, those that are determined by the underlying source traits. Altruism, dishonesty, curiosity, and foolishness are examples of surface traits. *Source traits* demonstrate the unity of the person. Dominance versus submissiveness, and ego strength versus neuroticism are examples of source traits. A scale developed by Cattell (1957), known as Cattell's 16 PF (personality factors) scale, measures source traits.

The main problem of any trait theory is that it gives a fragmented account of personality. Most traits are subject to environmental influences. Just because someone is aggressive on Sunday at the football field does not necessarily mean the person will be aggressive when he reports to work on Monday morning. Traits fail to predict the behavior of individuals across similar situations.

HUMANISTIC THEORIES

Various theories can be called humanistic, although they often are known by other names (for instance, existentialism). All humanistic theorists[2] posit that the core tendency of personality is to strive toward actualizing one's inherent potentialities. Actualization is tied to core needs (recall Maslow's need hierarchy). Life is a process of decisions, each involving an alternative associated with an unknown future and an alternative which allows the individual to revert to past routines. Anxiety and guilt are by-products of these decisions. For existentialists, a healthy individual is one who accepts this state of affairs, making future-oriented decisions and courageously dealing with the anxiety brought by these decisions. Man by nature is not aggressive and destructive. These traits are exhibited only when he is frustrated.

Humanistic theories of behavior stand in opposition to historic approaches, such as the psychoanalytical theories, which argue against

determinism in behavior. Freud believed that
the person's past psychological history determines his actual behavior. For him, childhood conflicts with parents were the causes
of actual behavior. Psychoanalytic theory
stresses the uniqueness of personality insofar
as it was determined by the person's unique
past history. Learning theorists of personality
(Dollard and Miller, 1950) also believe that
childhood reinforcement history shapes behavior. Humanistic theorists do not agree with
such determinism. What might differentiate
humanistic approaches to the study of personality from others is the stress put on the
freedom of the individual and the vigor with
which humanists oppose the dehumanization of
man. Humanists feel that man has an inner
self which guides his existence and is capable
of change. The self-determination view accepted
by humanists is critical of the idea of man as
mechanistically responding to rewards and
punishments, or as fixated on breast feeding.
A problem inherent in such a conceptualization
of the inner self as making decisions and having cognitive thoughts and aspirations about
the future, however, is the difficulty of
scientific measurement.

Humanistic personality theories espouse a
philosophical outlook because they deal basically with the notion of existence. McGregor
(1960) has been the most outspoken proponent
of this approach in his writings on organizations. Although not a personality theorist by
a longshot, McGregor's writings borrow heavily
from humanistic terminology. McGregor, in
terested in enlightening management on behavioral approaches, outlined two conceptions
of man, called Theory X and Theory Y. Old
style, authoritarian type of management is
based on Theory X, and assumes the following
premises about the nature of human beings:

1. The average human being has an inherent dislike of work and will avoid it if he can.

2. Because of this human characteristic of dislike of work, most people must be coerced, controlled, directed, threatened with punishment to get them to put forth adequate effort toward the achievement of organizational objectives.
3. The average human being prefers to be directed, wishes to avoid responsibility, has relatively little ambition, and wants security above all.[3]

The assumptions of Theory X are based on external control, and a deterministic view of man as lazy. McGregor refused to accept this pessimism and suggested instead Theory Y. Many ideas that appear in humanistic personality theory are included in Theory Y. The major premises are:

1. The expenditure of physical and mental effort in work is as natural as play or rest.
2. External control and threat of punishment are not the only means for bringing about effort toward the achievement of organizational objectives. Man will exercise self-direction and self-control in the service of objectives to which he is committed.
3. Commitment to objectives is a function of the rewards associated with their achievement.
4. The average human being learns under proper conditions not only to accept but also to seek responsibility.
5. The capacity to exercise a relatively high degree of imagination, ingenuity, and creativity in the solution of organizational problems is widely, not narrowly, distributed in the population.
6. Under the conditions of modern industrial life, the intellectual potentialities of the average human being are only partially utilized.[4]

When we recall Maslow's ideas on need

hierarchy, we can see that Theory Y follows in his footsteps. By allowing for a model in which man is self-responsible for personal outcomes and is creative and imaginative under the proper environment, McGregor draws attention to humanistic values in the organization. The only fault one can find with this approach is that it is more a philosophical statement on the nature of man than a theory of behavior. It has been customary to endorse McGregor's ideas in various texts of organizational behavior without requiring systematically collected data to substantitate them. Given the connotation and evaluation of Theory X against the background of our values, the preference given to alternative explanations such as Theory Y is understandable. McGregor's ideas have much influenced industrial humanists and their methods of organizational development.

STAGES OF PERSONALITY DEVELOPMENT

Most personality theories examine the way in which an individual unfolds and becomes a full person. The notion of the whole person has prompted many theorists to emphasize the mature individual as the unit of study. Nevertheless, because all theories stress the unfolding of personality, most have given attention to the process of development. In particular, psychoanalytic theory has stressed developmental stages in the life history of the person, showing how behaviors are affected with the passage to each stage. Other theories do not stress a notion of identifiable stages which the person goes through, but underline the importance of development from infancy to adulthood.

PSYCHOSEXUAL STAGES

Freud was a staunch believer in the importance of development. He traced the process from infancy to adolescence in four psychosexual stages, each identifiable with the sexual organs most prominent at that age: the oral, anal, phallic, and genital. Freud identified these stages because he felt that maladjusted people were fixated at the *oral stage*, when the baby depends on the mother for food. The *anal stage* reflects the beginning of toilet training; and fixation at this stage is represented by obstinacy, stinginess, orderliness. The *phallic stage* brings with it the understanding of sexual identity. The familiar Oedipus complex (where the son loves his mother) develops at this stage. After a latency period, the individual matures and attains the *genital stage* if he can form altruistic relationships with others.

Freud's terminology strikes many people as bizarre, ill chosen, and sex laden. As Mischel (1971) aptly points out, Freud was trying to conceptualize a learning process through which an individual progresses during his life at a time when no such conception was available in the sciences. A more neutral choice of words, such as dependent, compulsive, mature for the psychosexual stages might have obviated many of the myths and resistances which have developed around the theory.

Psychosocial Stages

Neo-Freudian theorists are characterized by their concern for giving social and cultural forces their necessary emphasis as determinants of personality. Whereas Freud was strongly tied to biological and psychosexual explanations, many of his students who broke ranks with him adopted a more psychological theory.

Erikson (1963) stressed the importance of the social adaptation which individuals have to make during development. He sees the person, from infancy, as faced with problems which he must solve and identified eight psychological stages of development each dealing with a psychological crisis. The way a child solves the crisis determines the kind of person he will grow to be. Table 8.1 shows Erikson's

TABLE 8.1 Erikson's Stages of Psychosocial Development.

	1	2	3	4	5	6	7	8
VIII Maturity								Ego Integrity vs. Despair
VII Adulthood							Generativity vs. Stagnation	
VI Young Adulthood						Intimacy vs. Isolation		
V Puberty and Adolescence					Identity vs. Role Confusion			
IV Latency				Industry vs. Inferiority				
III Locomotor-Genital			Initiative vs. Guilt					
II Muscular-Anal		Autonomy vs. Shame, Doubt						
I Oral Sensory	Basic Trust vs. Mistrust							

From *Childhood and Society*, 2d. ed. by Erik H. Erikson, with the permission of W. W. Norton & Company, Inc., New York, N.Y., Copyright 1950, © 1963 by W.W. Norton & Company, Inc.

psychosocial stages. The most important crisis
occurs at the stage of puberty and adolescence
with the gaining of identity and becoming an
independent, effective adult. Erikson believes
that many individuals postpone the identity
crisis to later years, when resolving it has
become more difficult. The stages prior to the
identity crisis allow the child to make identifications with the people who surround him.
However, as he becomes an adolescent the child
must outgrow these identifications. The
adolescent gains his identity from his experiences derived from experimentation with
different roles, occupations, and life styles.
Erikson says that, especially in urban Western
society, a moratorium period is allowed until
the identity is reached. Schools cater to
those who seek their identities, providing the
environment for the moratorium during which
the adolescent searches for an identity. Organizations may facilitate the solution to the
identity crisis because beginning a career
often signals the achievement of identity.
Furthermore, if the desire to produce is the
healthy attitude for young and middle adulthood, organizations seem to be adeqaute environments in which to resolve this crisis.

THE MATURATION CONTINUUM

Departing, in essence, from the notion of
strict stages, Argyris (1957) suggested that
personality is the unfolding of mature tendencies. There is a wide difference between the
characteristics of the child and the adult
which are reflected in development trends.
Argyris believes that some behaviors show distinctive changes from infancy to adulthood.
These changes are general to the population,
although each individual can express behaviors
in his own idiosyncratic manner. Table 8.2
shows the characteristics that develop from
immaturity to maturity.

Argyris sees this is as a descriptive model
of personality development, with self-actualizing

TABLE 8.2 Characteristic Changes in Individuals from Infancy to Maturity.

Immaturity	Maturity
1. Passivity	Activity
2. Dependence	Independence
3. Few behaviors available	Numerous behaviors available
4. Casual interests	Deep interests
5. Short-time perspective	Long-time perspective
6. Subordinate in society	Equal or superordinate in society
7. Lack of self-awareness	Self-awareness and control

Source: C. Argyris (1957), p. 50.

tendencies to be determined from profiles involving these characteristics. His notion of activity is closely related to Erikson's loco-motor-genital stage which has initiative as the crisis, and the notion of independence is associated with the autonomy crisis of the muscular-anal stage. He views these characteristics as continuous dimensions and the model supposes that all healthy human beings show these basic growth trends. This, in turn, suggests that organizations are staffed by adults who are active, independent, and able. The organization should provide the climate for further development of these dispositions. Argyris claims that organizations rarely take advantage of this information, and that many people are frustrated and experience conflicts between themselves and their organizations. There exists an incongruence between the character of the formal organization and the mature individuals who inhabit it. The organization expects passivity and dependence from the mature adult, thus making him regress to infantile behavior. This is not a healthy situation. The result has been that either these individuals have been kept from achieving their potentials, have become dependent, submissive, and passive; or they have been forced to strike, to restrict their output, or to absent themselves from the job.

DETERMINANTS OF PERSONALITY

An important issue for personality theorists is the nature-nurture controversy. This has to do with what determines personality. The evidence points out that the answer to this controversy lies partly in biology and partly in the environment where one grows up. In the following discussion of the determinants of personality we shall stress the importance of the situation itself.

BIOLOGICAL DETERMINANTS OF PERSONALITY

Although research by geneticists is inconclusive on the subject, it is believed that some dispositions may be inherited. Since chromosomes and genes are inherited, they should be responsible for certain behaviors. Under controlled conditions, experimentation with animals shows that certain physiological characteristics are inherited. The inability to conduct such studies with human beings restricts our capability to arrive at conclusions concerning the part heredity plays in the determination of personality because we cannot isolate the effect of the environment.

ENVIRONMENTAL DETERMINANTS OF PERSONALITY

The culture, the family, the group, and the

situations which make up one's environment
each influence personality. The culture dictates the values a person will learn and influences the common traits. Since the culture
dictates a good number of the acceptable behaviors, it reduces the variation in the behavior of its members. The culture's values
are transmitted by the family, which influences the children in many ways. Parents act
as models for many novel behaviors and reinforce certain attitudes. It is no wonder that
our personalities, in turn, partly reflect
those of our parents. Brothers and sisters also
influence personality. Sibling rivalry may
sometimes lead to maladjustments in the adult
personality. The interpersonal relationships
into which we enter also leave their marks on
our personalities. The extended family, the
peer group at various schools we attend, and
the formal and informal groups to which we be-
long in organizations can have profound effects on our dispositions.

THE INFLUENCE OF THE IMMEDIATE SITUATION. Personality theorists in general share the belief
that characteristics of the personality should
not necessarily be studied in respect to the
demands of the immediate social situation. Personality develops and stabilizes over time, and
for this reason one should be concerned with
the long-term effects of the environment.
Nevertheless, it is impossible to negate the
fact that the immediate social situation can
sometimes be very powerful, and dispose an
individual to behave in ways that a study of
his personality would not have predicted.
    The immediate situation can influence dis-
positions. Frustration, anger, and anxiety at
the work place can make the most docile,
active, and industrious individual aggressive,
withdrawn, or lazy. The compelling nature of
the immediate situation has been aptly demonstrated by Milgram (1965). Subjects were asked
to follow the orders of an experimenter and
give another person what they believed to be

strong electric shocks. Subjects were told
they were participating in a learning study
testing the effects of punishment on learning.
A confederate of the experimenter was the
learner and the subject was instructed to administer him a shock every time he gave a
wrong response to a test item. He was told to
start shocks at 15 volts and increase the level
by 15 volts up to 450 volts. Contrary to the
opinion of experts and many others, more than
50% of the subjects followed the orders and
administered shocks of 450 volts. A group of
psychiatrists, when asked to predict the outcome of the experiment, thought that only one-
tenth of one percent of the subjects would
administer the maximum shock.

Milgram's study shows that the immediate
situation can be very compelling, and reflects
upon the dispositions of well adjusted adults.
He suggests that we should study situations
more carefully in order to understand personality. Mischel (1973) strongly supports the
need to include measures of the psychological
environment of a person in order to understand
how a person makes discriminations. According
to him, personality consists not only of stable
characteristics but also of change in response
to the environment. He, and Bem and Allen (1974)
both propose that typologies of situations
and of individuals should clarify our understanding of personality. A person who acts
differently than his traits predict may not
necessarily be inconsistent but highly discriminative of situations.

THE CONCEPT OF SELF

Most personality theorists postulate an
abstract concept known as the self as being at
the core of personality. The *self* can be defined
as the image the person holds about himself.
This notion of self is influenced from infancy
on by the perceptions the person develops about
himself and the world around him. When we

discussed processes of attribution, we were
basically involved with the way in which individuals perceived themselves and others in
situations. The emphasis, as in the study of
the self, was with determining the dispositions by which people describe themselves and
the constructs they employ in describing
others. It would be difficult to delimit the
components of the self since the concept is
so elusive. Self-identity and self-attitudes
probably make up for most of the self.

The image we have of ourselves develops
through maturation, especially as we interact
with others who provide feedback data on the
behavioral assumptions we have developed about
ourselves. Cooley (1902) stressed the feedback
obtained in social interactions, using the
notion of the "looking-glass self." We reflect
our image upon others. This in turn suggests
the basic biases which enter into an understanding of the self. Others are selective
in what they perceive of us, and we in turn
can be biased in what we feel others think of
us. Since we have attitudes about ourselves,
we can conceive of these attitudes as having
cognitive, affective, and behavioral elements.
We have thoughts and feelings about our self,
and actions we take towards the self, such
as self-tolerance.

Following Cooley's lead, others have
elaborated on the fact that the concept of
self is developed by social interaction.
Rogers (1951) has shown that maladjustment may
result if a difference exists between the
perceived self and the ideal self. Anxiety,
self-hate, and an inferiority complex can develop from this state of affairs.

The self-concept is an enduring entity. As
people mature they develop a concept of the
self which shows little fluctuation. If we
conceive of everything and everyone with whom
we interact as our social system, at the center
of the system we find the self. The study of
the self was the traditional domain of
philosophy, but the realization that people's

awareness of their own image could be docu-
mented led to studies of what may be termed
the phenomenal self. The self is unique for
every individual and gives a picture of how
the various parts composing a personality have
been integrated into a whole. Defense mechanisms are also at the service of the self,
protecting it by denial and distortion of
reality.

SELF-ESTEEM

The self-concept has been studied in particular in regard to how it reacts with one's
sense of self-value. This field of inquiry is
known as *self-esteem*, a disposition by which the
persons represent positive and favorable aspects of the self-concept. A notion which has
received support is that people prefer others
who sustain their self-esteem (Harvey et al.,
1957).

Self-esteem as a variable can be manipulated.
In many everyday situations, people experience
feelings of self-worth or, in contrast,
feelings of letdown. We find sometimes that
we are not the person we think we are. Testing
the effects of dissonance and self-esteem,
Bramel (1963) found that subjects whose self-
esteem was inflated and who were then made to
believe they had homosexual tendencies, also
evaluated their partners in the experiment as
having homosexual tendencies. If one's self-
esteem is high, subsequent contrary information becomes dissonant and must be reduced.
Walster (1965) manipulated the self-esteem
variable by giving authoritative positive or
negative information to her female subjects
about themselves. When the subjects were
given a chance to affiliate, it was found that
those subjects whose self-esteem was lowered
tended to like affectionate people significantly more often than those whose self-esteem
was raised. Managers who can freely praise or
criticize the work of their subordinates can
influence the self-esteem of their workers.

In turn, some love and hate relationships in
the work place may develop as a function of
self-esteem. Dittes (1959) showed that when a
person has a strong need of approval he will
tend to like accepting persons and dislike
those whom he finds rejecting.

PERSONALITY MEASUREMENT AND THE STUDY OF TRAITS

Personologists frequently endorse the measurement aspect of personality. Some personality theories incorporate means of personality
measurement (for instance, Cattell's trait
theory). Most measurement techniques can be
applied to test assumptions of different
theories. The overlap in techniques suggests
that personality theories, too, overlap in
some of the concepts they use. The various
techniques developed for the measurement of
personality can be broadly categorized into
four areas: 1) Psychometric tests and scales
usually require the respondent to reply to a
structured questionnaire. Many traits have been
measured using psychometric measurement techniques. 2) Projective techniques have been used
predominantly to test assumptions of psychoanalytic theories, and less often to measure
traits. The guiding assumption in a projective
test is that the person projects onto the
ambiguous test his unconscious motivations. The
Rorschach ink-blot test, and the Thematic
Apperception Test are the best known examples
of projective tests. 3) Behavioral observation
relies on sampling the actual behavior of the
person to establish his reaction to the environmental consequences. This is more popular
with personality theorists who espouse a
learning approach. 4) Self-assessment techniques are favored for learning more about the
phenomenal self. Self-reports, interviews,
simple attitude statements (like the semantic
differential), and Q-sort techniques (Block,
1961) are used for self-assessment of personality.

The different measurement techniques of
personality each have their strong and weak
points. The important evaluation criteria are
how well they predict the traits they are supposed to measure. The reliability and validity
of the tests are very important notions that
should be consulted before accepting a test as
accurately measuring what it is supposed to
measure. To establish the validity of a test
we need a criterion against which to measure
the predictions made by the test. For example,
scholastic aptitude tests use actual school
grades as a validity criterion. Obtaining such
criteria for personality tests is very difficult. Therefore, most tests are not fail-proof
and no one test or combination of batteries
could yield a full and accurate picture of
personality.

We turn now to a representative list of
personality traits which has been studied. The
reader should keep in mind that most of the
research reported is of a correlational nature.
In other words, a scale is developed and used
to measure a trait. Then this trait is correlated to other personality dispositions.
No attempt to establish causality can be made
by such approaches. The ultimate test would be
how well the measured trait predicts behavior
in social situations.

AUTHORITARIANISM

Authoritarianism is a disposition characterized by submission to figures of authority
and conventionality, both social and political.
The post-World War II interest in understanding
fascism led to studies by Adorno et al. (1950)
known as *The Authoritarian Personality*. A Likert-
type scale, called the *California F-scale*, was
developed to measure the trait of authoritarianism, along with other scales to measure
anti-semitism, ethnocentrism, and political
and economic conservatism. The F-scale was
defined as a measure of antidemocratic trends
in one's personality. Conventionalism,

submission to authority, superstition and
stereotyping, and concern with sex were some
of the symptoms tapped by the scale. Authoritarians were described as being intolerant of
ambiguous feelings, having good opinions of
their parents and themselves, and projecting
and displaying their aggression toward easily
scapegoated minorities.

The F-scale has been widely used to find
what other traits are related to authoritarianism. Findings indicate that perceptual distortion (Scodel and Mussen, 1953) and sus-
piciousness (Deutsch, 1960) correlate with
authoritarianism. Vroom (1960) found that
authoritarians were not satisfied with
participating in the decision-making process
in organizations. This is a reflection of the
rigid character of the authoritarian. The
scale has been used in studies of prejudice,
leadership, and group conformity to see how
high and low authoritarians react in social
situations.

The various studies that have used the F-
scale have been criticized because of
methodological problems such as representative-
ness of the sample (Hyman and Sheatsley, 1954)
and acquiescence-response tendencies (Christie
et al., 1958). The concept of authoritarianism
measured by the F-scale has more recently been
criticized because the scale reflects cultural
values of the forties rather than more current
values (Marlowe and Gergen, 1969).

DOGMATISM

Rokeach (1954, 1960) has studied *dogmatism*,
which he defines as close-mindedness. His
studies are an offshoot of the authoritarian
personality studies. A dogmatic is a person
who does not accept information contradictory
to his beliefs. He has a simple cognitive style
characterized by dichotomous thinking, that is,
people are good or bad. Whereas authoritarianism is basically related to those having conservative political leanings, dogmatism taps

extremes of the right and the left of the
political spectrum.

In criticizing studies on authoritarianism,
Rokeach pointed out that the general trait of
authoritarianism was worth further study
rather than authoritarianism of the political
right only. He named this cognitive style
dogmatism. Rokeach (1960) developed a dogmatism
scale composed of forty attitudinal items that
correlated highly with the F-scale. In studies
it was found that dogmatics were more influenced by authority figures (Vidulich and
Kaiman, 1961) and were less liked by their
peers (Rosenfeld and Nauman, 1969).

MACHIAVELLIANISM

The ideas in Machiavelli's book *The Prince*
have influenced many political scientists, and
his description of a ruler has been taken as
the best example of a manipulator. Christie
and Geis (1970) have developed scales to
measure a disposition they call Machiavellianism. A Likert-type scale (the Mach IV) and
a forced-choice scale (the Mach V) are used to
measure this disposition. It is characterized
by a tendency to manipulate and to be detached
in interpersonal relations. The scales do not
correlate with the F-scale, suggesting that a
disposition different from authoritarianism is
being measured. Findings suggest that some
professionals such as psychiatrists are high
on the scale and surgeons are low. Many managers
would probably score high on a measure of
Machiavellianism.

ACHIEVEMENT MOTIVATION

Some personality traits are traceable to
motivational dispositions. McClelland (1961)
measured this disposition in a variety of
cultures using a projective test known as the
Thematic Apperception Test (TAT). What emerges
from the studies is that achievement motivation
is a trait of successful entrepreneurs and

businessmen. The high achiever in business is characterized as a calculated risk-taker who assumes responsibility for his problems and wants feedback on his decisions. Achievement motivation has been correlated with many behaviors and found to be an important trait. We refer the reader back to chapter 3 for a more extensive discussion of this trait.

EXTERNAL-INTERNAL LOCUS OF CONTROL

In discussing motivation and attribution theories, we singled out the dimension of external and internal locus of control. Rotter (1966) has devised a scale that has been used to measure this trait. The scale is designed to measure the extent to which an individual perceives that his behavior is controlled by himself or by sources external to himself. This perception is important because it generalizes to a perception of events surrounding the person. Studies have found "internals" and "externals" to behave differentially in the same situation. Internals are more independent and resistant to change. Reinforcements are tied closely to the perception of locus of control. An internal perceives reinforcement as the consequence of his own behavior, whereas externals feel they can have no control over reinforcements. Strodtbeck (1958) found middle- and upper-middle class people to be on the internal side of the dimension, and lower-class people on the external. Gore and Rotter (1963) discovered that internals were more willing to participate in civil rights movements than externals. The internal feels he can react to the environment and change the world as it affects him. The external lives in a world directed by fate. He does not make any efforts to change it. Sampson (1971) likens an internal to an entrepreneur and an external to a petty bureaucrat.

MANIFEST ANXIETY

The question of whether individuals tend to deal with their environment on an emotional level interested Taylor (1953), who devised a Manifest Anxiety Scale (MAS) to measure the extent to which anxiety responses are characteristic of an individual. Correlations have been obtained between individuals' MAS scores and observations of these individuals made by raters. Spielberger (1966) has distinguished between state and trait anxiety. MAS measures *trait anxiety*, which is a stable disposition. *State anxiety* refers to emotions displayed in response to the demands of an immediate situation. Those who have manifest anxiety would probably show a stronger response in any situation than those who only display state anxiety.

Anxiety is interesting to the organizational student because it can influence performance. Sarason (1961) found that high anxiety subjects, when threatened, do not perform as well as low anxiety subjects. Performance may sometimes be a function of how a task is presented. Managers should keep in mind that anxious people will perform just as well as those who are not anxious when they are not threatened by the task.

SOCIAL DESIRABILITY

An important problem for personality testing is the fact that people tend to present themselves in a favorable light. This is a notion we explained when discussing demand characteristics. The discovery that in experimental situations, subjects sometimes try to figure out what is being investigated and give responses they think the investigator wants led to devising indirect testing methods for attitude measurement. Personality tests also have this problem. People can deliberately

give answers which do not reflect their true
personality, thereby falsifying the information. There are two reasons for this biased
style of responding: first, the general content
of the questions asked; and second, the manner
in which questions are asked. Edwards (1957)
devised a test called a social desirability
scale by selecting items from a widely used
personality test known as the Minnesota
Multiphasic Personality Inventory (MMPI) to
measure the first reason. This trait taps a
disposition to respond to immediate cues of
the situation. Maladjusted people who display
social desirability answer questions as do
well adjusted and normal individuals. The scale
has a negative correlation of -.84 with the
manifest anxiety scale. Crowne and Marlowe
(1964) developed a similar scale to measure
the need for approval. They found that when
individuals have a high craving for approval
they tend to conform more to other people.

The manner in which questions are asked can
bring out an acquiescence tendency (Cronbach,
1942). People tend to agree or disagree systematically with test items. Couch and
Keniston (1960) called these two personality
types "Yeasayers" and Naysayers." It has been
found that Yeasayers have little control over
their impulses compared to Naysayers.

THE MANAGERIAL GRID

Blake and Mouton (1964) have developed a
technique known as Managerial Grid training
which has received wide application in organization development. The basic concept behind
the training package is the idea that organizational participants can be rated on how
strongly they possess two traits, concern for
people and concern for production. The interaction of these two dispositions is, in turn,
depicted on a two-dimensional grid, and five
typical styles are discussed. Figure 8.1 shows
in the authors' words the characteristics of
each type of management. The aim of the

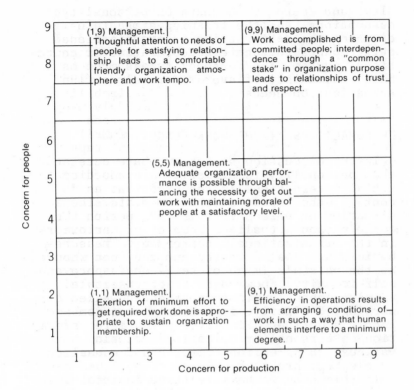

SOURCE: R. R. Blake and J. S. Mouton (1964), p. 10.

FIGURE 8.1 The managerial grid.

training program is first to determine, by use
of scales, where each person fits on the grid
and then follow a number of steps to modify
styles and change the behavior of participants.
The concern for production and concern for
people dimensions most resemble personality
traits, and they have also been identified in
various leadership studies as the two most
influential dimensions entering into the makeup
of a leader (Shartle, 1952; Fleishman, 1953;
Stogdill and Coon, 1961; Likert, 1963). As a
technique of organizational development the

Blake and Mouton grid rests on personality
assumptions, and the training aims at increasing the satisfaction of organizational
participants to secure a cooperative organizational system. The personality assumptions
have a humanistic flavor and revolve around
actualization needs.

PERSONALITIES AT THE WORK PLACE

In our discussion so far, we have stressed
that personality is primarily a product of
social interaction. In the organizational
context, the impact of the immediate social
situation on personality is very potent. The
whole person actualizes some of his behaviors
in the organizational environment. These behaviors are goal-directed and they contribute
to the person's image of self-consistency and
self-identity. Knowledge of personality gives
us clues about anxiety experienced while
working. Similarly, it can help classify
people's motives. Finally, appropriate information on personality helps in developing both
various job selection criteria and management
development programs.

In this book we have reviewed individual
behavior. We have explained behavioral processes that characterize the individual and
have emphasized the individual's involvement in
the interactive processes. In order to understand individual behavior in organizations,
it is also crucial to know the environmental
determinants of behavior. Interaction in groups
and membership in organizations cause effects
which modify an individual's behavior. He still
perceives, learns, and is motivated, but these
processes are to an extent shaped and modified
by his membership in various groups. In turn,
the study of interpersonal behavior will help
clarify the many assumptions we have developed
about the human being.

NOTES

[1]Those interested in personality theories can consult texts such as Hall and Lindzey (1970), Maddi (1972), Mischel (1971) for a thorough review of major theories.

[2]See Maslow (1968), Rogers (1961), Binswanger (1963), May et al. (1958) for more exposure on humanistic approaches to personality.

[3]Douglas McGregor, *The Human Side of Enterprise*, New York: McGraw-Hill, 1960, pp. 33-4.

[4]Ibid., pp. 47-8.

REFERENCES

Adorno, T. W.; Frenkel-Brunswick, E.; Levinson, D. J.; and Sanford, R. N. *The Authoritarian Personality*. New York: Harper, 1950.

Allport, G. W. *Personality*. New York: Holt, 1937.

Allport, G. W.; Vernon, P. E.; and Lindzey, G. *A Study of Values: A Scale for Measuring the Dominant Interests in Personality*. 3rd ed. Boston: Houghton Mifflin, 1960.

Argyris, C. *Personality and Organization*. New York: Harper & Row, 1957.

Bem, D. J., and Allen, A. "On Predicting Some of the People Some of the Time: The Search for Cross-Situational Consistencies in Behavior." *Psychological Review 81* (1974): 506-20.

Binswanger, L. *Being-in-the-World: Selected Papers of Ludwig Binswanger*. New York: Basic Books, 1963.

Blake, R. R., and Mouton, J. S. *The Managerial Grid*. Houston, Texas: Gulf Publishing, 1964.

Block, J. *The Q-sort Method in Personality Assessment and Psychiatric Research*. Springfield, Ill.: Charles C. Thomas, 1961.

Bramel, D. "Selection of a Target for Defense Projec
tion." *Journal of Abnormal and Social Psychology 66*
(1963): 318-24.

Cattell, R. B. *The Sixteen Personality Factor Questionnaire*, rev. ed. Champaign, Ill.: IPAT, 1957.

_____. *The Scientific Analysis of Personality*.
Baltimore: Penguin Books, 1965.

Christie, R., and Geis, F. *Studies in Machiavellianism*.
New York: Academic Press, 1970.

Christie, R.; Havel, J.; and Seidenberg, B. "Is the F-
scale Irreversible?" *Journal of Abnormal and
Social Psychology 56* (1958): 143-59.

Cooley, C. H. *Human Nature and the Social Order*. New
York: Scribners, 1902. Reprint. New York: Free Press, 1956.

Cronbach, L. J. "Studies of Acquiescence as a Factor in
a True-False Test." *Journal of Educational Psychology
33* (1942): 401-15.

Crowne, D. P., and Marlowe, D. *The Approval Motive:
Studies in Evaluative Dependence*. New York: Wiley, 1964.

Couch, A., and Keniston, K. "Yeasayers and Naysayers:
Agreeing Response Sets as a Personality Variable."
Journal of Abnormal and Social Psychology 60 (1960):
151-74.

Deutsch, M. "Trust, Trustworthiness and the F-scale."
Journal of Abnormal and Social Psychology 61 (1960):
138-40.

Dittes, J. E. "Attractiveness of Group as a Function of
Self-esteem and Acceptance by Group." *Journal of
Abnormal and Social Psychology 59* (1959): 77-88.

Dollard, J., and Miller, N. E. *Personality and
Psychotherapy: An Analysis in Terms of Learning,
Thinking, and Culture*. New York: McGraw-Hill, 1950.

Edwards, A. L. *The Social Desirability Variable in
Personality Assessment and Research*. New York:
Dryden, 1957.

Erikson, E. *Childhood and Society*, rev. ed. New York:
W. W. Norton, 1963.

Fleishman, E. A. "The Measurement of Leadership

Attitudes in Industry." *Journal of Applied Psychology 37*
(1953): 153-58.

Freud, S. *The Standard Edition of the Complete Psychological Works of Sigmund Freud*, 24 vols., edited by
J. Strachey. London: Hogarth Press, 1953.

Gore, P. M., and Rotter, J. B. "A Personality Correlate
of Social Action." *Journal of Personality 31* (1963): 58-64.

Hall, C. S., and Lindzey, G. *Theories of Personality*.
2nd ed. New York: Wiley, 1970.

Harvey, O. J.; Kelley, H. H.; and Shapiro, M. M. "Reactions to Unfavorable Evaluations of the Self Made
by Other Persons." *Journal of Personality 25* (1957):
393-411.

Hyman, H. H., and Sheatsley, P. B. '"The Authoritarian
Personality'—A Methodological Critique." In
*Studies in the Scope and Method of "The Authoritarian
Personality*," edited by M. R. Christie and M. Jahoda,
pp. 50-122. New York: Free Press, 1954.

Jung, C. G. *Psychological Types*. New York: Harcourt,
Brace and World, 1923.

Likert, R. *New Patterns of Management*. New York: McGraw-
Hill, 1961.

McClelland, D. C. *The Achieving Society*. Princeton:
Van Nostrand, 1961.

McGregor, D. *The Human Side of Enterprise*. New York:
McGraw-Hill, 1960.

Maccoby, M. *The Gamesman*. New York: Simon and Schuster, 1976.

Maddi, S. R. *Personality Theories: A Comparative
Analysis*, rev. ed. Homewood, Ill.: The Dorsey Press,
1972.

Marlowe, D., and Gergen, K. J. "Personality and
Social Interaction." In *Handbook of Social Psychology*,
vol. 3, edited by G. Lindzey and E. Aronson, pp.
590-665. Reading, Mass.: Addison-Wesley, 1969.

Maslow, A. H. *Toward a Psychology of Being*. 2d ed.
Princeton: Van Nostrand, 1968.

May, R.; Angel, E.; and Ellenberger, H. F., eds.

Existence: A New Dimension in Psychiatry and Psychology. New York: Basic Books, 1958.

Milgram, S. "Some Conditions of Obedience and Disobedience to Authority." *Human Relations 18* (1965): 57–76.

Mischel, W. *Introduction to Personality*. New York: Holt, Rinehart and Winston, 1971.

_____. "Toward a Cognitive Social Learning Reconceptualization of Personality." *Psychological Review 80* (1973): 252–83.

Rogers, C. R. *Client-Centered Therapy*. Boston: Houghton Mifflin, 1951.

_____. *On Becoming a Person*. Boston: Houghton Mifflin, 1961.

Rokeach, M. "The Nature and Meaning of Dogmatism." *Psychological Review 61* (1954): 194–205.

_____. *The Open and Closed Mind*. New York: Basic Books, 1960.

Rosenfeld, H. M., and Nauman, D. "Effects of Dogmatism on the Development of Informal Relationships Among Women." *Journal of Personality 37* (1969): 497–511.

Rotter, J. B. "Generalized Expectancies for Internal vs. External Control of Reinforcement." *Psychological Monographs 80* (1966): 1–28.

Sampson, E. E. *Social Psychology and Contemporary Society*. New York: Wiley, 1971.

Sarason, I. "The Effects of Anxiety and Threat on the Solution of a Difficult Task." *Journal of Abnormal and Social Psychology 62* (1961): 165–68.

Scodel, A., and Mussen, P. "Social Perception of Authoritarians and Nonauthoritarians." *Journal of Abnormal and Social Psychology 48* (1953): 181–84.

Shartle, C. L. *Executive Performance and Leadership*. Columbus, Ohio: Ohio State University Research Foundation, 1952.

Sheldon, W. H. (with the collaboration of S. S. Stevens and W. B. Tucker) *The Varieties of Human Physique: An Introduction to Constitutional Psychology*. New York: Harper, 1940.

Spielberger, C. D. "The Effects of Anxiety on Complex Learning and Achievement." In *Anxiety and Behavior*, edited by C. D. Spielberger, pp. 361-98. New York: Academic Press, 1966.

Stogdill, R. M., and Coon, A. E. "Leader Behavior: Its Description and Measurement." *Research Monograph No. 88*. Columbus, Ohio: Ohio State Univ., 1957.

Strodtbeck, I. L. "Family Interaction, Values, and Achievement." In *Talent and Society*, edited by D. C. McClelland. Princeton, N.J.: Van Nostrand, 1958.

Taylor, J. A. "A Personality Scale of Manifest Anxiety." *Journal of Abnormal and Social Psychology* *48* (1953): 285-90.

Vidulich, R. N., and Kaiman, I. P. "The Effects of Information Source Status and Dogmatism Upon Conformity Behavior." *Journal of Abnormal Psychology* *63* (1961): 639-42.

Vroom, V. H. *Some Personality Determinants of the Effects of Participation*. Englewood Cliffs, N.J.: Prentice Hall, 1960.

Walster, E. "The Effect of Self-esteem on Romantic Liking." *Journal of Experimental Social Psychology* *1* (1965): 184-97.

Whyte, W. H. Jr., *The Organization Man*. New York: Simon and Schuster, 1956.

Name Index

Subject Index